Barbara Toy was a well-known traveller and explorer. Elected a fellow of the Royal Geographical Society for her visits to Iceland, Yugoslavia, Greece and Lebanon, she later became the first Westerner to set foot on the summit of Mount Wahni in Ethiopia and received the Rover Award (an award granted only once before) for her transit of North Africa from the Niger River to the ᵗᵈiterranean. Described by Philip Llewellin as a 'traveller in the full-blooded sense of the word', Toy was the author of al acclaimed books, including *In Search of Sheba*, *A Fool c heels*, *Rendezvous in Cyprus* and *The Way of the Chariots*. S died in Banbury in 2001 at the age of 92.

Praise for Barbara Toy

A Fool on Wheels

'A highly-readable book about her solitary journey in a Land Rover from Tangier to Baghdad. A woman of remarkable courage.'
The Spectator

'She has a gift for people: she has an eye for places.' *The Times*

A Fool in the Desert

'Toy likes to travel alone. She has the gift for making us share her experiences. This traveller's tale is gay, intelligent and illustrated with sun-drenched photographs.' *Liverpool Daily Post*

'Lively and entertaining.' *The Times*

A Fool Strikes Oil

'A fantastic tale about a fantastic part of the world. The problems that have come to these countries through the headlong rush of riches are vividly revealed.' *Liverpool Daily Post*

Columbus was Right

'. . . describes her single-handed journey round the world with a Land Rover. In her light-hearted style she makes it all sound easy, and good fun.' *Daily Telegraph*

Tauris Parke Paperbacks is an imprint of I.B.Tauris. It is dedicated to publishing books in accessible paperback editions for the serious general reader within a wide range of categories, including biography, history, travel and the ancient world. The list includes select, critically acclaimed works of top quality writing by distinguished authors that continue to challenge, to inform and to inspire. These are books that possess those subtle but intrinsic elements that mark them out as something exceptional.

The Colophon of Tauris Parke Paperbacks is a representation of the ancient Egyptian ibis, sacred to the god Thoth, who was himself often depicted in the form of this most elegant of birds. Thoth was credited in antiquity as the scribe of the ancient Egyptian gods and as the inventor of writing and was associated with many aspects of wisdom and learning.

TRAVELLING THE INCENSE ROUTE

From Arabia to the Levant in the Footsteps of the Magi

Barbara Toy

TPP

TAURIS PARKE
PAPERBACKS

Published in 2009 by Tauris Parke Paperbacks
An imprint of I.B.Tauris and Co Ltd
6 Salem Road, London W2 4BU
175 Fifth Avenue, New York NY 10010
www.ibtauris.com

Distributed in the United States and Canada Exclusively by Palgrave Macmillan
175 Fifth Avenue, New York NY 10010

First published by John Murray in 1968

ISBN: 978 1 84511 995 9

A full CIP record for this book is available from the British Library
A full CIP record is available from the Library of Congress

Library of Congress Catalog Card Number: available

Printed and bound in India by Thomson Press India Ltd

FOR BILL

*'If you make no demands
then everything is a gift'*

I would like to thank the many people who assisted with permits, advice and their support; and the equally important ones who gave encouragement and help during the writing of the book, for without them the whole enterprise would not have been possible. I take the journey alone but they go every step with me.

Contents

Illustrations

All photographs are by the author

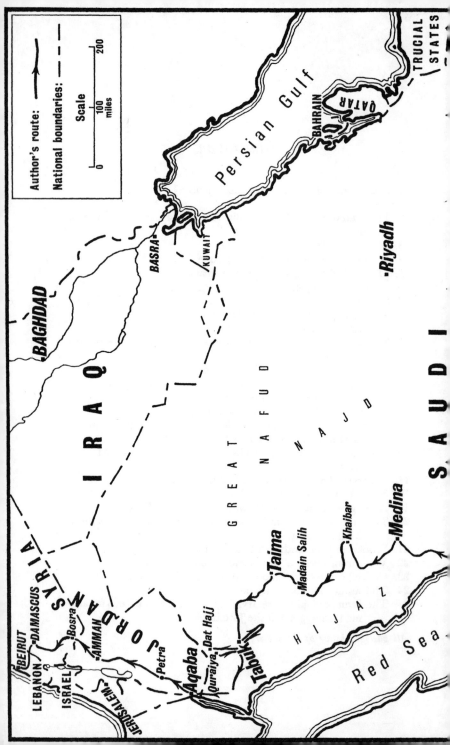

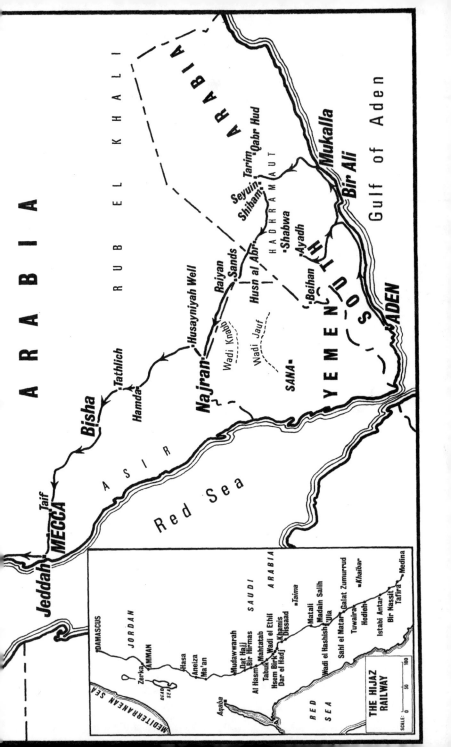

Prologue

THE SEA was opaque, spreading towards the Arabian shore without a ripple. I was sitting on the poop of an Arab dhow *en route* for Mukalla. My Land-Rover midships below, stood on bags of rice and around it other passengers, Arabs and Indians, leant against its sides with a proprietory air which was endearing. The sail stretched above to dizzy heights – as lethargic as we all were.

Beyond the shore, high basalt hills rose out of the sand, barren and a hard dying black. We were gliding towards a promontory that jutted out into the sea. Beyond was a perfect crescent of white sand that ended in a small walled village whose one gateway, a beautiful wooden structure studded with iron, opened direct to the sea as became the abode of fishermen.

'What is that place?' I asked the *nakoda*.

'The Bir,' he said, giving it the local diminutive.

'Bir Ali!' The Cana of ancient times. Near by two islands protect the inlet making it the best natural harbour along the south Arabian coast. For centuries it was the port and a starting point of the Incense Route that went north through the Arabian peninsula. Along its devious course was carried ivory, tortoise-shell, indigo, gold, pearls, diamonds and sapphires, silks and spices – all the treasures of Africa, India and the Far East – and most important of all the sacred and mystic frankincense which was precious beyond price, for without it who could be sure of a place in eternity?

How long the route had been in existence is not known for it was already a sophisticated highway that had made the country rich and earned it the name of Arabia Felix many centuries before the Greek Hippaius discovered the secret of the monsoon in A.D. 45. After this, with unfailing regularity they could sail across the Indian Ocean and, when the monsoon wind changed, sail back again. Thus the highway's trade was diverted as the northerners sailed direct and were no longer forced to pay the large dues demanded on the overland route. From then on the highway's importance gradually diminished and finally ceased when the belief and faith in the mystic power of incense no longer existed. The wealth that gave Arabia the name of 'happy' dwindled also and the grand highway together with the cities *en route*, were lost in the sand.

Somewhere beyond those black hills would be traces of the route that led from one city to another. What an adventure to follow it right through the peninsula to Damascus and the Mediterranean!

The *nakoda*, sensing my change of mood, glanced at me inquiringly.

'Do we drop anchor here?' I asked. He moved his head with a slight incline which is the Arab 'no'. 'No matter,' I said cheerfully, 'I shall return some time.'

'*Minshan laish?*' he was surprised.

'To go north – past Azzan where the Three Wise Men started from, through the Yemen, the Hijaz and on to Damascus.' I pointed to the black hills. 'To follow the way of the incense.'

But already his interest had wandered, for the regions beyond the coast were a matter of indifference to him. Maybe it was a fine highway thousands of years ago when his ancestors were great, but now it was desert waste; and he had the sailor's contempt for dry arid lands. However, he viewed me kindly, indulgently, for the British are an odd kind of nomad.

We glided on towards Mukalla. The great fisherman's sea door slid out of sight behind us and the sun threw lean shadows ahead. But now I was gloriously happy in perhaps the greatest happiness of all, that first realization of a new idea, a new plan. It was however some years before I could return to Bir Ali.

Unwelcome Traveller

The impossible we do at once –
miracles take a little longer.

I DROVE along the flat white beach east of Aden. I was
following a solitary lorry and marvelling at my good luck, for I
had been given permission to leave Aden and drive my Land-
Rover overland to Bir Ali three hundred miles along the coast.
As the track east scarcely exists we were using the beaches
whenever possible. There had been talk of bomb-plating the
Land-Rover's undercarriage and of travelling with sand-bags
under my knees, but finally – no doubt to be rid of me – they
sent me off with an Agricultural lorry. We could run over an
unlocated mine or bomb perhaps, but in principle the terrorists
were known to leave Agricultural lorries alone. We passed
Fadhli country which is still in the Western Confederation and
saw few people; the atmosphere was isolated and eerie; and we
drove on through the night to be away from the troubled
zones as soon as possible. Now, beyond the great black volcanic
headland lay Bir Ali!

My arrival in Aden, however, had been anything but welcome for the political situation was worsening every day and
few civilians travelled in the interior. I soon realized it was not
going to be easy to cross the territory or be given visas for other
countries. My first step had been to try and obtain a visa for
Saudi Arabia and to reach the less troubled East Aden Protectorate. The E.A.P. office in Aden lay past Steamer Point
and I was shown into a bare room with a large metal desk
and wired windows overlooking an open space covered with
tank traps. Behind the desk sat a young woman with an
intelligent face and beautiful hands. Her expression was
puzzled; I had come so unprepared, no Saudi Arabian visa,

no permit to enter the Yemen and not even permission to leave Aden.

'You should have written from England,' she said, 'it would have saved you the journey.'

'It is sometimes easier when one is on the spot,' I countered.

'There is no Saudi Arabian consul here and, as you must know, it is almost impossible to obtain visas for that country. You certainly cannot leave without one.'

It did appear crazy I had to admit. 'But I am often lucky about things like that,' I said, smiling warily at her youthful troubled face; 'would it be possible to ask our Embassy in Jeddah to help?'

She looked exasperated; there was a pause. But suddenly she smiled, 'Oh well, we shall see what we can do,' she said – and sent a signal to Jeddah.

An answer to the signal might take some time and while waiting I would try to follow the section of the Incense Route that lay in Southern Arabia. However, another incident nearly wrecked the journey before it had even begun for I was driving to ITTAHAD, the Administration headquarters in Aden, when the Land-Rover's engine began to miss. I drew to the kerb and stopped. To lift the bonnet which has a spare wheel on top is not easy. I am five feet two inches tall and reasonably strong, but it is necessary to put both hands under the bonnet flap, swing my body forward and under it, so as to give my arms the full support of my rigid straightened spine; and then with a big heave, jerk the bonnet upwards. This time it was my *back* not the bonnet that gave way, for the Land-Rover's front structure had been thrown out of true and it was stuck fast.

It took longer than I like to remember to climb into the vehicle, drive back to the hotel and reach my room. This misfortune would give the authorities a welcome excuse to refuse to allow me to continue, so no one knew about it until I left Aden. After two days I was able to move around, but I had become one of that vast army of people with fractured or weak backs, who previously I had treated with such scorn and boredom.

Now, as I drove over the black headland towards Bir Ali,

the rough surface made it necessary to change gear continuously and the effect of the accident was only too apparent as sharp pains went up my spine. I followed the lorry towards the brow of black rocks and below us lay the perfect crescent of white sand with Bir Ali shimmering in the haze beyond. The two off-shore islands, Dome and Isle of Birds, copper coloured and ringed with white guana, stood out sharply in the blue sea. A dhow made its silent way along the coast, just as mine had done ten years previously. I had finally returned!

What is atmosphere? Why does one house, village or strip of land have it; and why for one person and not another? Is it the perfect compliment that is truth and affinity for some people? Or is it greatness that becomes absorbed in the earth and even in people, so that they also have harmony? The stretch of white sand cut by black rocks, with the great mound of Husn el Ghourab immediately below, and edged by a sea of strident blue had an atmosphere that printed the whole scene indelibly on my mind.

There is however an abandoned air about Bir Ali today with its crumbling walls and empty houses. The sense of vitality engendered by full occupation does not exist, for the village is losing its young people and the pace set by the remaining ones is slow. Outside the village walls is a small fort with a tower room at one corner which overlooks the beach. It is used by travellers and the driver of the lorry, Salih, took me here.

'It is better you stay night here,' said Salih as we drew up in front of the iron doors.

The caretaker, a crinkled old man, ran ahead up the high steps leading from the inner court, indicating as we passed the toilet with hole in the floor and a large water jar. The roof formed a gallery overlooking the court and forts of this design are found all over the country.

No matter how sophisticated or accustomed Arabs become to European women, there is an air of relief when they can finally deposit them in a high room and put some old man or boy to guard and be within earshot. With evident satisfaction Salih watched me disappearing up the high steps before going on.

The old caretaker rolled up some straw mats and went off

with a goatskin to fetch fresh water, and I was left alone with a pain in my back that was reaching alarming proportions.

Moonlight has a strident effect in these parts, it brings landmarks nearer and gives them life. The crumbling village came into its own and the great mound of Husn el Ghourab encroached across the sand. The earth shimmered as though breaking through a dream of centuries. True, no craft of 'rafts held up by inflated skins' were making their way towards the shore, and no camels crouched waiting to be led by the bedu through the wadis and lower reaches of the Yemen mountains, Asir, Hijaz and finally along the King's Highway to Damascus.

That continuous stream, so old that donkeys made an even slower progress before the advent of camels, saw the rise and fall of many kingdoms along the way; the Minaeans, Sabaeans, Katabans, Hadhramaut and the Himyarites. Earliest records mention the Egyptians sending an expedition for incense in 2800 B.C. Some empires established colonies to the north to protect their trade and the Nabataeans in Jordan did the same as they penetrated *south* and established the rock-carved city of Madain Salih in Hijaz. Each kingdom, growing rich and ambitious, pushed farther south for they all sought control of the coastal areas and the forests of incense which lay to the east. The Minaeans whose capital was in Ma'in in Wadi Jauf, controlled the area from Najran to Wadi Kharid and they were forced south by the Sabaeans (of Sheba and Solomon fame) who in their turn made their capital at Marib with the famous dam which has left some of the greatest ruins in southern Arabia. To the east was Hadhramaut with its Holy City of Shabwa, the Sabota of Pliny, a sacred storehouse of incense as well as the junction of the routes coming west from the incense lands and also north from the coast. Lastly came the Himyarites with their capital in Safar near Yerim, who absorbed all the area to the coast, and were still in control at the beginning of the Christian era.

There is no doubt that in ancient days the caravans crossed these coastal mountains and converged at the south-west edge of the Empty Quarter (Rub el Khali). They went by the Thula Road from Cana (Bir Ali) to Azzan in Wadi Meifa'ah and so

north through Wadi Jerdan. Other routes passed through
Wadis Hajr, Amd and Do'an, joining the overland route from
Wadi Hadhramaut at Shabwa. From there they turned west
to Timna and Harib in Wadi Beihan and moved north through
Marib and along the eastern approaches of the Yemen
mountains to Jauf and Najran. At that time Wadi Beihan was
one great city and the remains of houses and temples, fragments
of exquisitely worked carvings and sculpture now lie in broken
heaps in the sand. This route, converging from Hajr, Azzan and
Hadhramaut, can be followed with certainty, but for centuries
it was closed firstly because of the decline of trade and secondly
when lawlessness and petty wars took over. The routes have
only been opened in this century when peace came to the areas.
If they were important centuries ago, they are doubly so today,
for whoever controls them and keeps them open, controls
southern Arabia.

I knew I could not take this route through Harib, Marib and
so to the Republican-held Yemen territory to Najran, for
once in Republican hands I could not pass into Saudi Arabia;
but as in previous times of war, the caravans are forced north-
east to Husn al Abr near the desert and so on to Najran, I
would do the same. It was a route taken later in Islam times
and today by the pilgrims to Mecca. My goal therefore at the
moment was Azzan in Wadi Meifa'ah, Ayadh, Shabwa,
Hadhramaut and Husn al Abr. If my visa for Saudi Arabia was
granted, then somehow the Yemen would have to be crossed.

As I pored over my maps and made my plans the Sultan of
Bir Ali's secretary arrived. He was a fussy young man in
European clothes and wearing steel-rimmed glasses.

'The Sultan is very ill but he has heard you are here and
wishes to see you,' he said.

We crossed the sand and climbed through a gap in the
village wall, crossing an uneven square towards the old sea
door. Originally the wall completely encircled the village and the
only entrance was by the doorway to the rocky shore, but such
precautions are no longer necessary. Near the door was a pair
of huge scales standing on a wooden platform. To the left was a
solid square building, quite unadorned, where the Sultan lived.
We passed through a high door which was opened by a heavy

rope worked from the floor above, and climbed the deep steps opposite. The walls were white with lime and had been polished. We removed our shoes at the first landing and entered a long room whose windows opened directly to the sea so that the sound of the waves filled the room.

The Sultan sat hunched up on cushions on the floor at the far corner. There was an echo of a tough, good-looking man in the shrunken frame and the firm line of the jaw, but now he was very old. A heavy rope with a noose-like loop at the end hung from a beam in the ceiling and the old man grasped it from time to time, hitching himself up as though he would hold on to life. His futah was crushed and he wore a dingy sweat shirt. A small white cap topped his grey face. There was a general air of disarray about him as though things were getting out of hand. Several men sitting on the floor along the walls nodded in a friendly manner as I passed. The old man held out his hand and his eyes searched mine with a desperate expression. What was he looking for? When told I was in the village he said I was his daughter returned at last. Had my arrival stirred some distant memory and had there been a special daughter in another land, whom he loved? His eyes held mine for a few seconds then his mind wandered and he sunk back, idly letting his hand find the rope again.

I shook hands with the company before sitting on a wicker sofa in the centre of the room and the Sultan's son, a plump boy of twelve, came over to talk to me. He wore steel-rimmed glasses and was more Indian than Arab. Such glasses are often worn whether necessary or not as they are believed to give the wearer a certain prestige.

'How are you?' he asked in perfect English, sitting on the sofa and agitating his knee in a characteristic Indian manner. He attended school in Mukalla where he learnt English.

We drank three cups of sweet milky tea and ate biscuits already soft in the humid air. There were men from Bal Haf along the coast and others from the interior, hard, wiry men with fierce black eyes who were contemporaries of the Sultan.

Until the last decade there was an old and fierce feud between the Sultans of Bir Ali and Bal Haf though both are branches of the Wahidi Sultanate. The Sultan of Bir Ali has

Camel Routes North

little territory outside his own village, although as he owns the best natural harbour along the coast he benefits greatly from customs fees. The Bal Haf branch live inland at Azzan in Wadi Meifa'ah and control far more territory. Twenty-five years ago the Sultans of Bir Ali successfully arranged for the assassination of the Bal Haf Regent, Abdulla bin Muhsin, a conscientious young man who worked hard for his small domain. The murderer was duly caught and retained as insane, and the Bir Ali Sultans paid a fine of Rs. 30,000 and then became more law abiding. They asked for a small government to be formed with the same advisory arrangements as the British had with the other sultanates.

There was also a group of elegant young men, three of them merchants' sons, a schoolteacher from Mukalla and the Sultan's 'doctor'. Their futahs were held up by modern belts made of canvas and leather, and European-style skirts hung loosely over the futahs. On their heads were kuffiyahs in light-blue, green or white which were arranged to very good effect. It is now fashionable for kuffiyahs to be edged with much larger white bobbles than previously.

The men plied me with questions: Had I been afraid in Aden? Where was my servant? Why didn't I have someone to drive the Land-Rover? Was I married and how many children did I have? The village, they found too quiet, but it was to Mukalla not Aden they wished to go. They spoke also of journeys north along the wadis. Although lorries and Land-Rovers pass along the coast and go north through some of the wadis, camels still carry much of the cargo.

'Which is the main route north to Shabwa?' I asked the older men.

With delight they fell into a wild discussion which disintegrated into noisy arguments and they illustrated distances by placing the right hand under the left elbow, a useful gesture which can mean anything from a few feet to a six weeks' journey to Mecca. In their opinion there was never one route but several and these changed with the situation, or during wars.

There are now two main camel routes leaving Bir Ali: one going north-east across the wilderness of Al Khabt to Dhiyeihi

9

country. It leads to the old Bana Wall, a passageway re-discovered by Von Wrede in 1843. The narrow defile is formed by the construction of a wall opposite the mountain cliff and built of shaped stones that rise to nearly twenty feet. The passageway is two hundred yards long and all approaching wadis and gulleys are blocked by masonry, thus it would have been impossible for caravans to avoid passing through, and to deviate when carrying the precious cargo was punishable by death. Along the rock-sides are Himyaritic inscriptions bearing witness to its use from early times. It leads to Wadi Hajr, the River Prion of Ptolemy, before turning north-west towards Shabwa.

The other route, the Thula Road, goes north-west to Rhudum and continues through Wadi Meifa'ah to Wadis Amaqin and Jerdan (The Godra Ptolemy) to Ayadh and on to Beihan. This route which I was taking would be more practical for camels for it has three wells on the otherwise desolate coastal plain.

'*Wallah!* I shall take you to Bana!' said a dark hawk of a man from Bal Haf; 'give me three days to collect camels and we shall be gone!'

'You will need permission from Mukalla,' said the Sultan's secretary pedantically, and this put a gloom over the gathering.

But my hawk-like friend was not to be side-tracked. 'Three days,' he repeated, 'and after you go to Meifa'ah in the Land-Rover and see *my* Sultan.'

The old Sultan sat dozing and we rose to go. He took my hand once again and there was the same searching look in his eyes. The old men watched with compassion as he sank back into an inner daze.

'It is unfortunate that I cannot go first to the Bana Wall,' I said to the secretary as we walked back across the sand to the fort, 'they are all very helpful.'

'It is their duty,' he said fussily. But it is something more than that, they enjoy an expedition no matter how small and if there is financial gain, then so much the better.

The freedom of travelling alone is dearly bought, and the lucky ones prefer to travel in a group, halving the risk and

Mubarak

sharing work and cost. The lone traveller is suspect to all but the Arab, who is fundamentally independent and has been conditioned to long periods of solitude. The idea however that all foreigners are people of substance still lingers and a westerner is expected to have an entourage, even if it is only a boy. Though part of one's freedom has inevitably gone, a good boy makes a journey more comfortable; but a bad one is utter disaster and the journey is lost.

Beside me sat a neat little man with greying hair, curiously round eyes for an Arab, and a toothless grin. Mubarak had been my 'boy' on the previous visit and he had contacted me again. He belonged to the Al Mudi tribe from Wadi el Aiser, whose male members all have the right to call themselves 'Sheikh'.

'What have you been doing all these years?' I asked.

'I drive a Land-Rover for the Indian doctor in Wadi Do'an and I am married and have a son.'

'*El hamdu lillah!* Just one child?'

He shrugged. 'Two – but other is bint.'

'Never mind,' I said.

'Where you go, memsahib?'

'To Jeddah, Damascus and Beirut,' I said optimistically.

'I come too.'

'And leave your family?'

'I send them money.'

'But I am going on to England, not coming back here.'

'*Tamam*, I come.'

'But . . . ' slightly exasperated, 'you wouldn't like that. It rains all the time.'

He looked disbelieving: 'All the time?' I nodded. 'Then it is good for your goats.'

'It is *very* cold,' I said severely, 'and the sun seldom shines.'

'*Wallah!*' but he was not convinced, 'I come too,' he repeated.

'Oh, you are a nomad, Mubarak! You are worse than I am.'

He gave me a toothless grin.

We sped along the coast which was already part of the outlet to the sea of Wadi Meifa'ah. The long stretch of isolated beach was crisp and clear in the early morning light, and as we drove thousands of gulls rose from the sand, flying just high enough to allow the vehicle to pass below before settling on the sand behind us again. We were driving beneath a huge billowing canopy of wings – unique and magical.

Ahead one solitary creature inhabited the entire beach; his small canoe made of a hollowed-out trunk and silver-grey with age was pulled up on the sand. Near by were rows of large king fish split and set out on the beach to dry. He was a Himyar, lean and without artifice. I scanned the high ridge of sand.

'You are alone?' I asked. 'There is no village here?'

'No village,' he confirmed and his gaze moved to the beach stretching east and west and to the wide sea horizon; he paused a moment then glanced down at me. 'Alone?' he queried, with a wide sweep of the hand.

I laughed suddenly, happy for this quiet solitary person and as we drove off I glanced back. He looked like a king.

I was becoming efficient at beach driving and bridged the soft sand approaches with no trouble. It is better to keep as near the water's edge as possible, but storms can make deep ingrains up the beach so that suddenly there is no space between the water and a high bank. This calls for a split second decision – into the water, or rushing the high bank and the possibility of toppling over. To stop would be disastrous and many lorries have stuck and been swept out to sea on the next high tide.

The track leaves the coast and goes north into Wahidi country towards a line of brown hills called Humatri. On rising ground a cluster of palms surround the wells of Rhudum and beyond lies the village itself. The waters of the wells are very sweet and all travellers stop to fill their goatskins as they have done for centuries. There are sulphur springs in the village where it is possible to stand in steaming hot water and inhale the fumes which, they will tell you, are good for rheumatism and chest complaints.

Wadi Meifa'ah stretches like a great wide estuary far into the interior; its broken sandy surface is interspersed with strips of higher ground ridged by flood waters which come from the hills far out of sight. Sturdy acacia bushes grow along the sides and silt which has piled up making precarious strips of fertile ground cultivated by the local people. We floundered often, running towards chaotic churned up sand mounds, and several times were forced to retrace our steps.

In the hills to the east live the Himyars whose ancestors formed the last of the great Arabian kingdoms, and in the wadi itself are sections of the Qateibi who have a long and bad reputation for highway robbery and brigandry. The area is the confederation of the 'Abd al Wahid, 'The Slave of the Lonely One', which is the eastern border of the district known as the Mushreq, the 'Eastern Land'. Even to the east in Hadhramaut they still refer to the territory as the Mushreq.

At last a raised flat neck of land in the centre of the wadi came into view; it was the village of Meifa'ah. Several square white buildings were occupied by the administration personnel and the local police. Beyond was a small line of tiny shops made of mud bricks which formed the suk. The offices of the Adviser were on the ground floor of one of the buildings and wide dark stairs led to the living quarters above. The ceilings were high and the rooms spacious with a large colonnaded veranda running along two sides of the building. Massive blinds of rush matting turned the veranda into a lounge with dining alcove. The long line of Jebel Rhubar ran along the western side of the wadi and to the east the ground fell away to a far, broken horizon.

James Conway, the Adviser, was extremely tall and he regarded me mildly and with an air of someone used to just *anything* arriving up the high dark stairs. 'I received a signal that you were coming,' he said.

'There is a rest house here?' I asked.

'It is in need of repair,' he said, 'but I have an extra room.'

The bedroom was painted green for coolness and had a bed enclosed in a vast mosquito net. Salih, the house boy, took one look at me and put a large pot of water on the fire; a hot bath, it seems, is the first prequisite of any *nasrani*, male or female.

Life in all administration set-ups is punctuated by 'signals' and in small Adviserates they are very conspicuous and control the existence of those in charge. They arrive from headquarters as well as from other remote posts, at all times of the day and night and with demands, reprimands and cryptic questions and answers. Those from the outlying posts are often dramatic, needing immediate attention and action, so that suddenly and at any hour the establishment bursts into hectic activity. Previously I had become caught up in these dramas, sitting up in bed, fearful as to whether we were being attacked or that yet another piece of the Empire was about to fall; but now I have learnt to slip my head under the pillow and continue my night's rest.

There is also a continuous stream of callers – for to be inaccessible makes one suspect. As well as the Emir, the Qaid, Sheikhs and their secretaries, there are ordinary locals, and the wandering bedu bringing tales and complaints; and above all the various V.I.P.s who may drop in by plane to 'view the situation'. Conway answered signals, gave advice, listened to tales and served tea with calm imperturbability.

Night brought a certain uneasiness and few people left their homes after dark. Dining that evening on the veranda I realized the importance of the rush matting which shielded us from the blackness outside, for without it we would have been an easy target. How soon would it be before more organized terrorism moved into the valley? There was a sense of urgency and I decided to press ahead in case the situation deteriorated.

'Is it possible for me to continue to Ayadh?' I asked Conway as we moved from the table.

'Oh yes, you can go ahead,' he said.

'I gather the authorities would want me to take a guide from Ayadh, past Shabwa and on to Wadi Hadhramaut?'

'Yes, but that could be arranged through a signal.'

'There would be no difficulty?'

'None at all, it is just a matter of finding a good guide.'

'It is rather frustrating to be so near Beihan and not to see it,' I said finally.

'You could go across from Ayadh and have a look,' said Conway, 'the Sherif of Beihan's lorries come all the time.'

I was surprised. 'They told me in Aden it was not possible to go overland to Beihan.' There had been several sorties from the Yemen into Beihan territory and the track was reputed to be continuously re-mined.

'I shall send a signal,' said Conway.

The Beautiful Wife

'Oh, thank you! I suppose the situation seems worse to the Adenis than it does here.'

At this moment there was a commotion in the passageway and Salih came in, he spoke to Conway in rapid Arabic.

'It is as well you were not at the Rest House,' said Conway to me, 'for the roof of the bathroom has just fallen in!'

Next morning Ali, the Adviser's second-in-command, accompanied me to the local school. In the crowded class-rooms the boys looked clean and intelligent. The advanced class was having an English lesson when we entered; the boys regarded me silently, their faces withdrawn and inscrutable and as we finally left the room a slow hiss followed us out.

'It means nothing,' said Ali, ever eager to please.

He left me when I called on the chief clerk's wife who came from Aden. She was very beautiful with honey-fair skin and an oval face, and she wore an effective long blue velvet dress with several beautifully worked gold necklaces and bangles. Blue chiffon embroidered in gold covered her head. The plainness was unusually attractive and probably owed much to Aden sophistication. We had tea, a picturesque ritual at which she officiated with grace and *savoirfaire*. Towards me she was a little superior for I had no gold, husband or children but she inspected my clothes thoroughly and tried to visualize my life, having none of the shut-in mentality of the ordinary wadi women.

On my way back I passed a group of Subians who were making mud bricks. They are the descendants of the Abys-sinians who overran Southern Arabia from the third to the sixth century A.D. They were finally conquered in A.D. 560 and having been conquered *invaders* are considered even lower than slaves. They greeted me cheerfully; one was digging sandy soil from a hole near by whilst another mixed it with water and handfuls of straw. A third placed a square wooden frame on the ground beside a row of finished bricks and then poured the mixture into the frame. With a practised hand he smoothed the surface and quickly whisked the frame upwards and away. The brick was left with the others to be baked by the sun.

Unwelcome Traveller

An older man in the group suddenly asked me for 'bach-sheesh' and the others looked shocked and disappointed as though the demand put me apart from them.

'*Bachsheesh?*' I queried, 'ah, *shukran!*' and held out my hand.

Taken by surprise, the old man delved into the folds of his tattered shirt and produced a small coin. When I took it, with many thanks, they were all delighted and the old man rose to his full height, acknowledging my thanks with dignity. I have it still, it links me with the Subians of Meifa'ah.

2

Over the Jol

Time and I against any two.
– PHILIP THE SECOND

WE STOOD at dawn outside the Administration building. Conway's Land-Rovers were just moving off, he had received a signal instructing him to proceed immediately to the eastern border to settle a dispute amongst the tribes. The area could only be reached, first by Land-Rover and then by foot. Was it mere coincidence that a contingent of Aden Levies had driven noisily into the village the previous night and set up camp conspicuously near by in the wadi? Things seemed to be hotting up and I was pleased to be moving off whilst it was still possible.

The wadi was held in mist as we started off. The yellow sands, spiked with stunted bushes, were enveloped and still. The solitary sound of the Land-Rover's engine fell heavily into the sand as we headed up the wadi. Between Mubarak and myself sat Salim Islam Haufily, a cheerful askari who was returning to his unit in Wadi Amaqin. He had been instructed to show me any ruins or inscriptions *en route* – anything that could give a clue to the ancient path through the wadi. Intent on his duty he instructed me to turn off to the right after we had been driving seven miles. We bumped over rocky ground and ahead of us was the large and imposing sight of the pre-Islam ruins of Naqb al Hajr (Maipha Metropolis). They stand on a high mound enclosed in a fine city wall of large limestone blocks with two gates facing north and south respectively. Squared bastions are set at regular intervals along its entire length. It is one of the few walled towns in southern Arabia, Shabwa and Timna being the other two of note, and it is an imposing sight silhouetted against the skyline as it rises out of the wadi.

Over the Jol

We left the Land-Rover and climbed to the south gate where the wall which is six feet thick is completely intact. Farther along, the inner face of smaller stones has been stripped away for more recent building purposes. In the east face of the gate is a long inscription giving the name of the town as 'Maifat' by which the wadi is known today. The gateway is free from sockets for doors or drawbridge, and there is no sign of a lintel, either of wood or stone. The north gate is less imposing and has been narrowed by building a wall against the existing face and great limestone slabs have been placed in the entrance, thus raising the ground level. There are signs of more than one attempt to rebuild or reinforce the walls at this point. Floods are a hazard in terrain such as this for it can rain on the jol miles away, sending flood waters through dry country which arrive without warning.

There is the remains of a tower to the south-west corner and the inner site is divided by a small valley running north and south towards each gate. West of the north gate is a stone-built well or tower, exposed by erosion and flood waters and near by the remains of the only buildings in the inside valley. On both the east and west hills are the ruins of buildings which have also been stripped of their outer face. Outside the walls are the remains of tiny square structures, graves perhaps or used by the people of the caravans, and later by pilgrims.

As yet there is no evidence for dating the site, and surface sherds and pottery are very scarce, though the buildings as they stand are believed to date from around the first century B.C. However, with such an imposing position it is reasonable to suppose the site was inhabited long before this time.

We returned to the wadi track and came immediately to an ancient narrow passageway built of stone and cut through a small hill where it would be necessary for camels to pass single file. Here were indications of the need to check caravans as they passed from a city.

Ahead of us was Azzan, standing high on uneven ground which gives it a precarious air. The mud houses cluster together around the Sultan's palace like a gigantic ant-hill. The windows, ringed with white, stared at us and heads showed for seconds between the crenellated edges of the *rheims*. A few small boys and two young men dressed in plain indigo futahs with magnificent *jambias* stuck in their belts, answered our questions with guileless directness. Their skins, stained from the cloth, gleamed like gun-metal in the bright sunlight. The Sultan was away in Aden and they pressed us to stop for tea.

The sun-drenched scene was vivid and still; the pile of buildings, the unattended palms stocky and leaning at odd angles, the indigo men, sons of Qateibi, the ibex antlers above the beautiful wooden palace door and the clear eyes of the small boys below me. It was from here that the Three Wise Men began their journey to follow the bright star to Bethlehem with their tributes of gold, frankincense and myrrh. And it was around here also it is believed, that three hundred years later the emissaries of the Empress Helena came searching for 'Sessania Adrumatorum' – the Azzan of today. They found the bones of the Magi and took them to Constantinople where they stayed until later taken to Milan, and finally in the twelfth century to Cologne. Had the Magi passed through the narrow defile we had just left, on their way from Naqb al Hajr and had they stopped here at the well as we were doing, I wondered?

Later we continued along the wadi seeing few people; the country was undisturbed for the activity engendered by authority in Meifa'ah and Azzan had scarcely penetrated here. There was more harmony between the people and nature, for the rhythm was the same, evolving through the centuries, when even violence meeting violence was fulfilment, for each knew the other's worth and the victor won. Soon the pace will change, as the people move faster and the unease of transition begins.

We pulled up at midday in the shade of a vast overhanging rock. The wadi spread out in front of us, a hard glare coming from the myriads of smooth white boulders which filled its base. Between the stones grew acacia, tamarisk and *ishr* (Calotropies) bushes. The latter with its large grey-green leaves and small white flower grows in every desert wadi, it is poisonous to animals but used between rafters when building houses.

We sat brewing tea and eating tinned salmon, cheese and

dates with some of the heavy local bread. A bedu woman in blue-black gown, following a herd of goats moved down the wadi. Salim called to her and she replied cheerfully until catching sight of me, she stiffened, stopped and said something which, roughly translated, meant: 'Christian, go home!'

I stood up and walked towards her; she regarded my approach with hostile, startled suspicion. '*Salaam alekum!*' I said.

She scowled, her startled eyes full of hate. Her dull black gown fell in folds to her ankles and was held up with an embroidered belt from which hung a silver chain. A heavy silver armlet encircled her wrist and she carried the branch of a tree.

'*Tamam,*' I said, indicating the bracelet.

She scrutinized my face, with the shrewd assessment of a child. I smiled into the searching eyes that had already begun to lose their viciousness; and then she smiled, becoming suddenly shy, and uncomfortable in her shyness.

I was the first European woman she had seen and the only white person other than those who whisked by in a vehicle. Yes, she had heard about the British and was surprised at my obvious harmlessness. '*Homra,*' she murmured at last as though this was the answer; and then she was off after her retreating goats. I watched the black figure moving over the stones, flickering in the heat haze. There must be hundreds of similar women in the country who listen regularly to the anti-British propaganda on the radio and who will never meet one of us.

The track climbs out of Wadi Meifa'ah and runs across the Ba Sardah – a dreary upland of black volcanic rock and entirely uninhabited – and drops into Wadi Amaqin, an intimate little wadi enclosed in the high watershed of the jol. The few buildings we passed were set against the cliff sides and the banks were reinforced with solidly made walls of stone. Bunds directed the waters which came from the surrounding jol into small levelled and enclosed plots that lay along each side of the wadi. There was no track but lorries had dug deep into the stones of the wadi bed and we were in danger of being straddled on the mound.

A Guest of Sheikh Ali

Ahead at the bend in the wadi was the village of al-Raudah. A picturesque fortress-like building rose above the others, its three storeys tiered and recessed to a final high tower. It was the home of Sheikh Ali bin Mahammad bin Fahaid who, as we drew near, appeared and moved down the slope, futah fluttering and accompanied by an animated group of small boys.

'*Ahlan wa Sahlan!*' he said, his round face beaming a welcome. He insisted that we were his guests for the night.

We left the Land-Rover in a cul-de-sac behind the Sheikh's house and passed through an outer court which was knee deep in straw; a camel eyed us distantly as we passed. The Sheikh pushed open a heavy door and we were in a completely dark hall. We groped our way up deep stairs to the first floor where light seeped through from the *maglis* ahead. From the stairs above came the familiar sound and flutter of the harem which was just out of sight around the curve in the stairs. The Sheikh's *maglis* had carved wooden pillars down the centre and a line of windows with ornate filigree shutters that let in shafts of light. Alcoves in the thick walls held torches, playing cards, a child's ball, pencils, a radio and a shell-like Chinese tea set. Bright patterned linoleum covered the floor and hard oblong cushions were set against the walls.

News of our arrival spread quickly and as we sat leaning against the hard cushions, villagers came straggling into the room. They spoke with a curious rush of words, followed by a sharp intake of breath. Sheikh Ali's face revealed his opinion of each visitor and when they asked too many questions about my journey he registered disapproval, signalling to me behind their backs not to answer. Finally, he could contain himself no longer and he beckoned me out of the room.

'It is not good,' he whispered, 'to tell them your plans; where you are going.'

I promised to be more discreet. Was this a hangover from the times when one needed a *siyara* (a representative of the tribe whose territory one was passing through), or had the 'emergency' penetrated into this peaceful valley?

The household was stirred to great activity and from time to time servants came in to whisper in the Sheikh's ear. It is a disconcerting custom, for the murmur behind cupped hands could have more sinister implications than whether there are enough eggs for tea or if little Ali should go and borrow the Naib's tablecloth.

Loud music came from a transistor and we tried to speak above it. Questions directed at me were difficult to hear and my answers, I hoped, equally so; for the Sheikh kept me under stern surveillance. Finally he beckoned me out again.

'*Homra!*' he whispered and led me into a tiny room off the *maglis*. Five women sat on the floor with their backs to the light. In one corner were piles of rugs and tin boxes, and a camel saddle was propped up near by. I sat opposite the women, our knees almost touching. They were animated and excited, fluttering their headscarves, whilst the bangles on their pretty wrists made a tinkling sound. They could have been a row of brightly coloured birds on a bough. For some reason we all spoke in whispers with a great air of conspiracy though we could not be overheard. The main spokesman was an older woman with a strong face and an assured manner who was the Sheikh's first wife. She was dressed in flowered cotton on a black background and wore a black headscarf. Two young women plied me with questions about Aden, for although they had not been there many male relations had. They both wore figured silk dresses and rows of silver necklaces and their fingernails had been hennaed. The eyes were heavily made up with khol and green lines ran from lip to chin. Two of them had a fancy design on their foreheads. The third girl was in her teens, her oval face was smooth as old ivory and her fine hands lay palms-up in her lap. She had the stillness of assured beauty and sat inscrutable as a young Buddha. She regarded me with surface interest as one would look at a planet through a huge planascope. Beside them and hovering round to pass the teacups was a tiny slave dressed in contrast to the kaleidoscope of colour around her, in faded black; but her eyes sparkled and she was full of enthusiasm and interest, joining in the conversation and exclaiming forcibly with a great rush of breath.

All the women sat cross-legged and their knees fell away loosely with the suppleness and ease of those who always sit on the floor. Some tucked one leg beneath and bent the other knee in front clasping it, which is the nearest position most Europeans can accomplish with any degree of comfort.

Before long they forgot to whisper and having found out I was not a doctor, their interest waned. My lack of husband, children, or even jewellery made me only half a woman. Finally they rose to go, climbing through a minute door in the back wall, whispering again and departing in excited secrecy. The Sheikh and I returned to the sterner problems of inquisitive bedu and the radio.

A very old man joined the company. He wore an indigo loin-cloth and carried a huge wooden stick. His hair hung in loose curls to his shoulders and a piece of cloth was wound round his head making a jaunty crown. He was a Bil 'Obeid and came from the beaches of Wadi Irma.

'I was in Wadi Irma ten years ago,' I said, and he nodded as though he knew. 'It was a long trek, through Shabwa and into the Rub el Khali.'

'*Wallah!*' His eyes were merry. He said he had accompanied Van der Meulen on his trek across the jol from Ayadh to Hadhramaut, but it seemed impossible that he could be so old.

Suddenly over the radio came Nasser's voice. The conversation stopped abruptly and everyone sat motionless listening. This is a ritual no one dare interrupt and as the voice went on, the company became more and more hostile towards me. With each new accusation (against the British) I was regarded with increasing gloom. Even my new friend from Wadi Irma watched me resentfully from below his fringe of curls. Perhaps it would have been better to camp in the wadi after all.

Finally the voice stopped and the whole company relaxed and were soon chatting again.

Dinner was served in the tiny room off the *maglis* where a plastic cloth had been spread on the floor. There was a large enamel dish of saffron-coloured rice with small onions, eggs and chunks of meat, surrounded by bowls of hot spicy sauce with onions and tomato which we sopped up with pieces of the flat rough bread. We used it also to wrap portions of meat or rice. The meal was delicious and we ate a vast quantity. Our host beamed with pleasure as he kept pressing food on us. When we could eat no more, the dishes were taken away and tinned pineapple brought in. Most meals are eaten quite quickly and there is very little conversation. Finally back in the *maglis* coffee was served.

The tiny room was cleared once more and hard cushions and a heavy eiderdown placed on the floor, for it was to be my bedroom for the night. Through the small door at the rear was a bathroom with a huge earthenware jar of water, a drop lavatory and some soap. Gone are the days, not so long ago, when soap was considered bad for the health.

Sheikh Ali handed me a torch, taking a final look round the room. 'You will be safe here,' he said, 'we shall sleep in the *maglis*.' Then with a slight nod towards the other room where the company was still chattering, he whispered, 'Please – not to "Flit" too loudly!' and he was gone.

Sheikh Ali accompanied us along the wadi next morning, as far as his territory extended, for custom dies hard. He climbed out of the Land-Rover on to the rocky wadi bed, stick in hand, the folds of his futah fluttering in the brisk morning breeze. His jovial round face was smiling and contented as befits the perfect host, and with a slight raise of the arm he set off towards a group of houses on the left bank.

Salim had been instructed to continue with us as far as Ayadh and having become reconciled to me as a driver, he hoped to come all the way to Beihan. Mubarak sat gloomily between us, he was tired and disgruntled for he had been guarding the Land-Rover the previous night and tried to sleep in the high Dormobile roof bed.

'But, Mubarak,' I said, 'the bed is beautifully comfortable!' *I* had spent an extremely uncomfortable night on the hard floor.

'But it is too far from the ground!' he wailed, 'I was in terror that I would sleep – and fall out!'

Aqaba Rahwan, the high pass leading across Jol al Mahjar to Wadi Jerdan, is a fine engineering feat although already some of the steeper sections near the wadi bed have been washed away leaving large exposed stones and neither maintenance nor repairs has been carried out. Several times we were forced to use the Land-Rover's four-wheel-drive. As we climbed higher the road wound round the hills leaving deep chasms below. At the approach to one of these Salim motioned me to stop.

'*Laish?*' I was annoyed for it would be difficult to start again on the steep decline.

'We walk from here to the top,' he said, 'you go on.'

The road was not *that* steep or narrow: '*Laish?*' I repeated.

'It is better,' he said non-committally.

Mubarak's eyes were showing white, a sign he was nervous. I shrugged. 'Oh, all right,' I said, and let in the clutch.

The road was wide and well surfaced, though there was a slight camber towards the cliff edge and I moved slowly to the summit where I waited for my companions curious to learn the reason for their behaviour. They came slowly towards me looking slightly shamefaced.

'Just what is the matter with that stretch of road?' I demanded, 'and why is it dangerous?'

After much hesitation and with gestures measuring from hand to elbow the story came out. Some months previously a lorry coming down this particular stretch of the pass had crashed over the side and the occupants had all been killed. And again, three weeks ago, another lorry belonging to the Sherif of Beihan had crashed at the same spot. The driver, curious to see where the other lorry had overbalanced, went too near the edge and crashed himself. He and four of the passengers were killed and eight others dangerously injured. The spot was becoming the haunt of a *jinn* and no self-respecting Arab could be expected to drive past it.

The high plateaux of Southern Arabia are deceiving at first glance for they appear bleak and stony with little or no vegetation; but plants are hidden amongst the stones; *dhorur* and *ra*, which are boiled and used against dysentery, and small posies of blue flowers, a diminutive replica of the large *solenostemma oleifolium* found in the centre of the Sahara. The eye becomes accustomed to other marks, footprints as it were, left over the centuries. Along one skyline were mounds set at regular intervals and made of large flat stones placed without plaster. As to their purpose or significance even the bedouin do not know, though they tell you the 'disbelievers before Islam' put them there. Perhaps they were used for defence or as a signpost for travellers; the latter is most practical for the stark skylines all look alike and without a track it can be easy to lose one's sense of direction. There were remains of paved ways leading up the cliff sides telling of transport wider and much more important than the camel; and everywhere those faint indentations which cover the jol like a cobweb – the camel tracks that link the wadis with each other.

We were forced to repair the road before the final descent into Wadi Jerdan for the track had been swept away by floods and the Land-Rover was in danger of toppling over; and once on the flat we ran immediately into a fertile little glen where trees and shrubs grew abundantly. Over the stones, tiny rock plants formed a mat of blue and the shrubs were in full bloom making a kaleidoscope of vivid yellow, pink, blue and purple.

This is Arabia! This is the desert where one endures the barren stony jol and the harsh weather, but suddenly, generously it gives such a resting place, or a well of sweet water; or a sunset that turns the end of the day of sandstorms and wind into an evening of great beauty.

Wadi Jerdan, the Gorda of Ptolemy and territory of the Bil 'Obeid was, until the last decade, little known by those outside its territory. The wadi lies between the east and west areas of southern Arabia, leading north into the desert and it is sur- rounded by turbulent tribes. Its inhabitants, however, are a cultivated and settled people, and many of them travel, going as far as Europe, America and the Far East. The beautiful wadi has been famous for its honey since the first century and the architecture of the houses rivals that of Hadhramaut, with the added advantage of not having been spoilt by modern trends.

It is narrow at the south end of the wadi so that the cliffs appear higher and each curve of the deep and cultivated valley reveals one beautifully proportioned building after the other. The houses are high and each one is a fortress, tapering in fine proportions to the final roof, where from its centre, rises a slender tower which is a diminutive but complete replica of the whole house. Each corner of the roofs or *rheims* have raised points giving a stylized effect. Windows are sparse and nonexistent on the ground floor, which was necessary in previous times when sieges were an ordinary occurrence. A long funnel, similar to a wind channel, runs down the wall from the roof to the first floor. It is used as a speaking shaft to visitors below and leaves the occupants out of sight. Wives can also drop the key to the outside door to their husbands when they return home. Around each house are *ilb* and acacia trees growing to enormous heights and beneath most of the trees are patches of green lucerne and durrah, enclosed in low mud walls which are expertly built and have the same raised corners as the houses. They give the whole wadi a professional, finished appearance, like an extremely well-kept garden.

We passed several crumbling ruins all too eroded and flood-swept to be of interest and came to two villages facing each other; al-Nuqaiyib on the left and al-Jaif on the right. As we drew level the Land-Rover stopped. The jolting had dislocated a lead from the distributor and as we fixed it several boys and men came from the villages to watch. This was the spot where the traveller Van der Meulen camped thirty years ago and despite the escort of a *siyara* there had been angry scenes that nearly ended in tragedy. Now the mild-looking men watched us at work, far more interested in the Land-Rover's engine than in me.

The Sayyids of Markha, the Manqad, tribal judges of ancient Mushreq, come from this valley. The Chief Manqad is elected from one family and he then chooses five others outside his own family and with them sets up a court of appeal. Their final judgements are given according to Ash Sharias Al Ada and Al Haq (the Holy Law, Tribal Custom and Truth) and their judgement, once sought, is law. Once a case has been put to them, the tribesman abides by the decision and should he fail to do so he forfeits his honour and brings great shame on his family. The Manqad always go unarmed and they dress extremely simply. Their power is declining but they are treated with great respect.

The sides of the wadi are strongly reinforced by stone walls which protect the terraced fields from seasonal floods. Some of the walls are very ancient but they have been carefully repaired and maintained. There is a continuity between the people and the wadi; the expertly constructed walls, the fields carefully and systematically cultivated, the houses in which they live and store their grain, show life as it has been lived for centuries.

There was no doubt also as we advanced and the wadi widened that it had been the scene of much greater activity, for everywhere there were signs of water conservation and the ruins of communities larger than those remaining today. Opposite the village of Ash-Shiqq are the ruins of al-Bureira, once an important town built of stone and an ancient caravan post. Five miles to the west are the ruins of al-Banna which are of more recent construction although the lay-out is the same with a large oval enclosure and gates at each end. We climbed over the crumbled mounds of al-Bureira where the stone is half covered by mud and silt. Here, as at Naqb al Hajr the gates are completely open and, spreading like a fan to the south are the remains of an intricate system of irrigation. Everything had been done to conserve and use the seasonal rains; the cisterns, the irrigation weirs and the *tissu* which are cut into the rock and enclosed to preserve the water from evaporation. If they were made to work today the whole valley would be green and fertile again. It is not difficult to visualize the outcome for the outlines still remain – like a skeleton fallen into the sand. What a scene would have confronted me two thousand years ago should a caravan have been approaching from the coast! A shuffle behind me made me turn. An old man with a sack grinned up at me.

'*Hajr?*' he shook the top of the sack that lay beside him.

I looked at the stony landscape around me. What would I want with stones? '*Minshan laish?*' I asked.

He slid his lined old hand into the sack, sought with care and withdrew it holding a chunk of stone which had been roughly broken. Across the levelled face was finely carved Himyaritic script. I was shocked. Somewhere near by was a fine inscription which was being crudely mutilated.

'Where did it come from?' I asked, indicating the landscape with my hand.

A crafty look crossed the lined face and his whole body dissolved into one large shrug. He had no intention of telling me but produced other pieces broken from lintels and pillars.

Arrival at Ayadh

'*Faloos!*' he demanded, holding them up.

I was not going to encourage such vandalism. '*Musch tamam!*' I said but he grinned and shouldering his sack, went off across the rubble.

The wadi was flattening towards the desert, the low line of Jebel ad-Diss lay to the east and there was now little cultivation, though small herds of goats grazed amongst the stunted bushes.

'Ayadh,' said Salim, pointing ahead.

The horizon had become a flat grey line broken by a series of low buildings and three watch towers with a flag flying from the highest. They were the squat mud buildings of the desert oasis, thrown up from the surrounding sand. To the north-west was the rounded mound of Jebel el Milh (The Salt Mountain) whose old salt mines are still being worked, and beyond lay the desert of the Ramlet Sabatain. To the north-east was Shabwa and the great wadi of Beihan lay north-west.

The noise of the solitary Land-Rover driving up the wadi had been noted by askari and inhabitants alike and a crowd was waiting outside the fort as we drew up. We shook hands with several of the elders and a group of bedouin stood silently by, they wore indigo cloths with heavy silver armlets encircling the upper arm and some had a jambia stuck in their belts. Their hair was long and curled loosely around faces that were almost hairless – giving them a deceptively feminine appearance. These were the Qaramish, a small tribe who mine and export the rock salt which is still considered the best kind by most Arabs and the mining of it is the cause of their sallow skin. The Qaramish, I had been warned, are *miskine*, they are unpredictable and unreliable.

Luqmoosh the officer in charge was a turbulent and handsome young man, tall and dark with wild black eyes. He instructed me to drive the Land-Rover in front of the fort doors where a guardian would be in charge of it.

Mubarak looked round darkly at the onlookers, 'The people of Ayadh are not good,' he said gloomily, as he followed me into the fort.

We moved up the deep steps to the tower room. From the ramparts there was a good view of the village and Jebel al Milh.

'That is where the salt comes from?' I asked.

29

'More than salt,' said one of the soldiers cryptically.

'*More* than salt?'

He nodded triumphantly, 'We shall find oil there – when the British leave.'

My Arabic was too sketchy to embark on such a tricky political argument. The presence of certain fumes in the vicinity has led to these rumours.

Many of the villagers followed us into the small tower room where the radio transmitters took up most of the space. Luqmoosh motioned me to sit on a narrow strip of matting which lay along the outer wall. He called loudly for tea, pushing many of the inhabitants out of the room. The radio operator had the round bland face of a Yemeni and he was trying to repair the transmitter.

'Where you go?' asked Luqmoosh, regarding me with an odd look of triumph which I could not understand.

'To Beihan,' I said. 'I have been told you will arrange a guide for me.'

'Not possible,' he said in his boisterous way.

I had a sense of misgiving. 'Why?'

'Read,' he said, putting a signal in front of me and grinning triumphantly.

There was silence whilst I read the signal. It instructed me to return the way I had come! And go to Mukalla.

'It is not possible,' I said, 'I cannot go back. I shall signal Conway and tell him so. There must be some mistake.'

'No mistake,' said Luqmoosh. 'No civilians allowed to go overland to Beihan.'

'They told me that in Aden, but Conway said . . .'

'It is what Aden says . . .'

'Oh, I know. Oh well,' I switched my thoughts to stifle my disappointment, 'I shall go straight on east to Hadhramaut.'

'Not possible,' said Luqmoosh and the radio officer in unison.

'Why not?'

'Signal says you must return the way you came.'

'But there was never any doubt about my going *east* from here,' I said, exasperated. 'On my previous journey I came here from Husn al Abr via Shabwa.'

'I Shall Leave to Go Back!'

As I looked at their faces I knew it was hopeless. I saw the long trek back, the stony wadis, the impossible Aqaba. My aching back would never survive all that jolting again. The prospects and the disappointment were too much. I looked out of the window towards the desert, fighting to control myself. The company, seeing my struggle, had ceased to chatter and even Luqmoosh's air of triumph was deflating.

'You signal Conway?' he suggested.

If their triumph at my misfortune had been disturbing, their solicitude was almost worse to bear! 'Please,' I said, moving to the bench near the radio.

It was not easy, for when we contacted Meifa'ah, though I could hear parts of their speech, they could not hear me at all.

'It is better you do question and answer in Morse,' said the operator. And so we started.

'*Is that Meifa'ah? I want to speak to Conway.*' A pause.

'*Please speak.*'

'*I know it is impossible for me to visit Beihan. May I revert to original plan and go east to Hadhramaut?*'

'*No. Instructions you return this way.*'

'*It is impossible. My vehicle will never climb Aqaba Rakwan again.*'

'*Is your vehicle U S ?*'

'*No, but I would not guarantee its safe arrival. The journey across the sands this way to Hadhramaut is flat and easy.*'

'*You must return this way.*'

I was becoming annoyed for it was stupid. I knew the track from Ayadh to Hadhramaut via Shabwa was easy and also was well out of the danger zone. I signalled again.

'*I do not think it is possible.*'

'*Then wait and I shall come for you.*'

This shook me. It was far too dramatic and emotional for a person as calm as Conway. Why was he suddenly so intense, so concerned for my safety? It was certainly not the effect of my blue eyes! Had things really become dangerous, or were just about to blow up? If a man as busy as he was contemplating coming all this way . . .

'It is no good,' I said to Luqmoosh. 'I shall have to go back.' We turned to the radio again. '*Shall start for Meifa'ah in the morning. If not there within three days send for me.*'

Over the Jol

'*I shall certainly come.*'

What was I driving back into? Just what was going on in Meifa'ah?

'Come,' said Luqmoosh kindly, 'we look at the salt mines.'

*   *   *

To return defeated is a low, dispiriting experience. I felt like the Roman, Aelius Gallus, whose expedition to Marib had been sabotaged by the Nabataean King, and had I been so betrayed? Also, my position was disturbing, for such a set-back can snowball. In a country so riddled with the signal system I was as conspicuous as a newcomer in an English country village and once people begin saying 'no' it is easier than saying 'yes'. Salim, who had previously regarded me as a composite object of person-cum-Land-Rover, now realized I was female and therefore vulnerable, thus subject to emotions and moods. If I could have shown my unhappy feelings further by emitting the *zaqharit*, that trilling sound made by his own women in times of stress, the illusion would have been complete. He regarded me with a bland stare, trying no doubt to conjure up in his mind my other existence, my life beyond this long and tiring journey. In Wadi Amaqin we said the usual staid Arab 'good-bye', enlivened a little by his surprise and pleasure at my gift of money, and then I turned the Land-Rover's nose to the wadi bed again and Mubarak and I bumped down the valley towards the high aqaba, alone.

Mubarak accepted the change of plans with native fatalism and without comment. We had been badly treated but it was Allah's will. When we came to the disaster spot on the aqaba he stayed with me in the Land-Rover even though it was more dangerous to drive *down* the track than it had been to come up! When we reached flat ground we smiled at each other.

'I am a good *jinn* you know, Mubarak,' I said. 'Maybe from now on that part of the road will be safe.'

'*Tamam*,' he said as though he believed it. Perhaps these roving *nasranis* had their uses after all.

To my intense surprise all was quiet at Meifa'ah. There was no emergency, no drama. Conway had not even returned from

32

the border and it was the gregarious Ali who had received the Aden signal and been ready to leave at a moment's notice to come to my rescue!

'My God!' he said as I came in, 'you are back! You are safe? *El hamdu lillah!*' and his charming face crumbled with relief.

'Oh, Ali,' I said, 'I thought that at least we were at war.'

'War?' A minor occurrence obviously. 'Thank God you are safe!' he repeated. 'What now?'

Well might he ask! I shrugged. 'I shall go to Mukalla, and afterwards . . .' For it is a very thin thread by which such a journey hangs.

The retreat continued and by the time we finally limped into Mukalla the vehicle was in need of extensive and expensive repairs; which proves that damage and accidents to vehicles occur when their drivers are either tired, in pain, depressed – or all three.

3

Mukalla

A curious sensation, to delve into one's past; one is inclined
at times to ask whether the record can be authentic.

NORMAN DOUGLAS

PREVIOUSLY I had arrived in Mukalla by dhow, dropping
anchor off-shore and facing a double row of salmon-coloured
hills, with four little white forts on the summit and the town
with little space because of the hills spreading along the water's
edge – like a curling breaker along the shore. The small white
customs house topped by a fancy balustrade on the quay was
surrounded by an avalanche of cargo. Busy craft were bobbing
about and being paddled furiously, and one of them took me
ashore because it was too choppy for the dhow to go alongside.
Dozens of little dark men in brilliant futahs, turbans and perky
jambia, and the neat little Indian harbourmaster who coped
with me and the crowd and sent me off in procession through the
high gates along the main street to the Residency.

It was the same main street but crowded now with Land-
Rovers used as buses, and Mercedes Benz, which is the general
choice for taxis. Horns sounded at the pedestrians, donkeys
and occasional camels who moved as slowly as always. The
road to the harbour gates was made precariously narrow by
piles of wood off-loaded from a dhow. A cheerful guard waved
us through and we drew up outside the customs shed. As I
climbed the three steps into the bustling main office a young
man came towards me.

'Good afternoon,' I said, holding out a paper of identity.
'My name is Barbara Toy.'

'*Ahlan wa sahlan*,' said the young man, glancing past me to
the Land-Rover. 'You have been here before,' he continued,
'but that time your Land-Rover was smaller.'

He must have been one of the innumerable small boys who untiringly begged a lift. 'You have a good memory,' I said.

'Yes. Do you stay at the Residency?' he inquired.

'No, I have been given permission to stay at the Shell Company Rest House,' I said.

'Times change,' he said, to which I agreed.

Changes had been slower here than in most countries and Mukalla was still a small town with one main street and a few alleyways beyond. The Sultan's palace, a frightful Indian-Victorian structure, was unchanged, whilst opposite, the Residency had been painted white and lost its sombre ochre charm. In the compound were buildings for the residency staff and the old blue and white palace was soon to take on hotel status. The increased traffic in the town now warrants a policeman to control it through the city's one gate to the west and outside in the wadi a modern petrol station has been added to the camel park. But the magic of the untouched has already gone.

The Shell Company's storage tanks lie three kilometres east of the town at Sharif. The local Shell manager and his family occupied the ground floor of the Rest House near by but he was away and his wife, who was in purdah, welcomed me behind closed doors. On the floor above was a large bedroom, a sitting-room, bathroom and a terrace with a fine view of Mukalla across the water. Below the terrace an awning of straw matting covered a half-finished dhow, and five stray dogs, healthy and well fed on a diet of fish guts and heads, played around its hull. The setting is beautiful but it is soon to go for there are plans to turn the point into a wharf for heavy cargo. The colour of the cliffs changes with the light, becoming gold and bronze towards evening, and making a fiery back-cloth to the town's white buildings and minarets.

A boy from the compound brought eggs and tea prepared in the kitchen below, '*Ahlan wa sahlan!*' he murmured, placing the tray on the terrace as the lights of Mukalla, now electric, sprung into life, ringing the minarets and blinking on in a disjointed fashion all over the town.

Mukalla is the capital of the Qaiti State, the largest and most important of the Sultanates of the East Aden Protectorate and its area extends inland across the jol to Wadis Hadhramaut and Do'an. The older Kathiri State, once more important is now confined to the eastern portion of the great wadi and the area north to the desert.

Previously the whole area consisted of a series of small sultanates, some with as few as twenty members, who were perpetually at war with each other. Every man carried a gun and most households in the wadis were fortified with their own dugouts leading to the family's plot of land. In 1933 Harold Ingrams of the Colonial Office, accompanied by his wife, arrived in Aden and some months later was sent to Mukalla, having been given the task of trying to make peace amongst these tribes; an undertaking which succeeded beyond anyone's expectations. It was surely the kind of opportunity and adventure all men dream about. 'Angrums' and 'Doreen' are still remembered with esteem. Except for a few lone travellers they were the first Europeans to penetrate into the interior. They travelled rough, often by foot or donkey, visiting the numerous tribes. The pacification of Hadhramaut and the bedouin tribes of the jol led to the creation of East Aden Protectorate and with 'Ingrams' Peace' came the desire in other areas for peace and like treaties. Let us hope his great effort has not been entirely in vain.

The Residency, stark in its coat of white paint, was dull and withdrawn and the present Minister, quiet and shy. It was fortunate that Jim Ellis was in charge of the northern region; he is the type of European whom Arabs trust and admire, being big, well-mannered, soft spoken and scrupulously fair. He has been in the country many years and knows the people well. Few such people remain, for with the disintegration of the Colonial Service the personnel is depleted and very mixed. Some are filling in a few years before final retirement, whilst others come from Kenya and other countries now ruling themselves. Many of the latter are young men bitter against Britain and not the best people to have in troubled areas. They scoff at their predecessors, discounting their efforts and nothing that was done previously has any worth.

Jim Ellis saw no obstacle to my going north to Wadi Hadhramaut, though he did not believe I would be granted a visa for Saudi Arabia. That the war-wrecked Yemen lay in between was something we did not mention at the moment. If the Saudi Arabian visa *was* granted I could then go north to Husn al Abr, which is the last desert post from Hadhramaut before the Yemen and as I had made the journey from Ayadh, through Shabwa to Husn al Abr previously, the entire route from Cana on the coast would than have been covered.

There are two tracks across the jol to Wadi Hadhramaut and we took the eastern one as on the previous journey. Then, it had been a desolate trek across the high plateau which separates the wadi from the sea, with few lorries. Now heavy traffic has turned the surface into a badly corrugated and dangerous track. Huge vehicles came lumbering towards us on the narrow pass and others blocked the way having stopped with a puncture, a breakdown or even to make tea. In some of the gulleys pockets of cultivation were the only signs of any population at all.

We were returning to the part of the world thought by many and certainly by the Hadhramis themselves as the most ancient. It is their belief that they are the descendants of Joktan and that their tribal ancestors were giants. The long tombs of the prophets Hud and Salih still exist in their wadis and these were the work of the sons of Ad who lived for over a thousand years. Who can dispute their beliefs for the Bible, whilst telling of the sons of Joktan, is silent about what happened to them afterwards. We know, however, that after the Addites there came Amr, called Hadhramaut, and later when this tribe split up, the descendants of his brother Yararub became known as the people of Kinda. The two tribes fought continuously for supremacy and finally the Kinda kings were victorious, and the Hadhramis became bedouin. The Kinda kings ruled until a disciple of the Prophet came to convert the tribes to Islam and there followed several invasions. The Yemenis who overran the country in the thirteenth century ruled for three hundred years until the Kathiris rose to power under their leader Bedr Bu Tuweirak. El Bedr reinforced his army with mercenaries from the Turks, the Yafa'i and the Zeidis of the Yemen so that the blood of many nations runs in their veins. After a further invasion by the Yemeni, they in turn were finally ousted by the Yafa'i whose descendants became the Qaitis. The more recent struggles between the older and more powerful Kathiris and the Qaitis has a musical-chair quality; with the Qaiti finally emerging as the most powerful of the two. It is only in the last decade and since Ingrams' Peace that the two states have worked in harmony to the mutual benefit of both.

We spent the night at the police post at Raidat al-Ma'arah on the high jol. The two askaris in charge cleared the tower room for me and shared our evening meal. Mubarak produced better meals when we were on the road and the more people there were to share it the happier he was. With the help of two pots and my tiny Swedish petrol stove he prepared a fine meal of rice with crisply grilled fish, a hot spicy sauce of chillies and another of onions and tomatoes, as well as freshly baked chipati-like bread, which he made on a shallow iron dish we had bought in the Mukalla suk.

The sergeant belonged to the Hummumi tribe, which is one of the largest in these parts. They are mountain men who live east of the road and towards Mahra country. Even today the Ba Hassan Ba Tunbul section are the sole growers and exporters of betel nut; a fascinating reminder of monopolies as in the case of the tribe of incense gatherers.

Mystery and a great sense of mystique surrounded the gathering of the incense, which was jealously guarded in a procedure that was strictly a ritual. One portion of the tribe only was allowed to gather it and they practised complete abstinence from any wordly contact during harvesting. It was treated with reverence and the demand for it was boundless. The Egyptians in early times believed that unless one was embalmed in incense there was no chance of eternal life, and it was also used at all functions, on every altar and at funerals. Rooms were kept sacred for the purpose of storing it and Pliny speaks of 'a single gate being left open for admission into the city of Shabwa'. To deviate from the highroad whilst carrying it was made a capital offence and as dues were paid to each person who handled and guarded it *en route*, its value, as it made the two thousand miles journey north, rose six hundred per cent.

The Incense Lands

And where exactly were these incense lands? The whereabouts of the actual forests has become a guessing game which all travellers to these parts play, for each finds a new wadi which fits in their mind Pliny's description: ' . . . a place situate on a lofty mountain (Shabwa). At a distance of eight stations from this is the incense-bearing region . . . inaccessible because of rocks on every side, while it is bounded on the right by the sea, from which it is shut out by tremendously high cliffs. The forests extend eighty miles in length and forty in breadth'. This area undoubtedly included the lands of Hadhramaut and Dhufar to the east. No doubt the incense in Hadhramaut was taken overland to Shabwa, whilst that of Dhufar came by ship to Cana for the coast we had just crossed from Cana to Mukalla and farther east was for centuries considered not only dangerous but unhealthy.

Some bushes of incense still grow in the side wadis, though it is not collected to sell for commercial purposes; a little, however, is still burned and it is sometimes used in water to purify it. The trees are tapped from March to August with a small incision cut into the bark as one would a rubber tree, and the milky juice takes three or four days to dry according to the heat of the sun. Many ancient writers speak of the sacred tree, Herodotus mentions the winged serpents that guard it and the tree spirits that follow along the caravan route, guarding the sacred drops taken from their sides.

All night lorries stopped outside the iron gates of the fort that banged each time the askari went out to check the passes. The still quiet nights of previous times had gone; Arabia Felix was reawakening.

Next morning we came to Wadi Hadhramaut near the village of al Ghuraf – a cluster of houses set behind mud walls and shaded by palms. Directly opposite, the north cliff ran east and west and an air-sock was flying in the wadi bed, which is used as a landing ground. To the west are the two main oases of Seyuin and Shibam and to the east, past al Ghuraf the wadi bends and becomes indeterminate as it leads to the holy city of Tarim, the home of the famous Al Kaff Sayyids.

A new granite road leads to Seyuin and runs down the centre, by-passing several villages along the wadi sides. Far to the right is Bor, a group of little villages of the Al Bajari who claim to be the descendants of the original inhabitants of the wadi. To our left there came into view two white buildings joined by many steps, for one of them is set high up the cliff side. It is the monument of Sayyid ibn Isa al-Muhajir from whom the Hadhrami sayyids are descended, and is now a place of pilgrimage especially for women. We turned off the road and bumped across the sand towards it.

The sayyid was born in Basra and after making the pilgrimage to Mecca came south to the ancient town of al Hajarein in Wadi Do'an. Later he moved east to Wadi Hadhramaut where he found a group of the Moslem sect of the Ibadites whom he fought in order to convert to the more orthodox belief. He settled here and having a great love of gardens helped to make the valley as beautiful as it is today.

The buildings and the long stairway were shining white and clean. There was nobody to be seen. The shrine was small with a domed roof and a plain whitewashed tomb, and near a tiny room for ablutions. To the west of the buildings rose the long stairway, pristine as though no mortal foot had touched it; it rose, pearly white up the cliff side. What pictures it conjured up of remembered tales from childhood; it was Jack and the Beanstalk and the Stairway to Heaven all rolled into one! We left our shoes at the bottom in deference to the unsullied white-ness and climbed to a ledge where there was a building I could not enter and an antechamber with mats, a coffee pot and cups left for pilgrims. Whether it is authentic historically or not, it is held in awe as a holy place and certainly the Holy Sayyid succeeded in founding the privileged class of sayyids who were the direct descendants of the Prophet by his son-in-law and daughter Fatma. These holy men whose influence and status has naturally lessened in the modern world, served an important purpose, for their holiness, impartial judgement and immunity in unsettled times had a restraining influence.

As we watched, an old woman came swiftly up the steps, running her finger along the wall, for she was blind. She was the custodian. It was a good place, she said, after greeting us; it was peaceful. She moved around with sure steps for there is little bric-à-brac to disturb her. And finally she came back to me. Had I come to pray? Women came all the time, she said, to pray for sons. No, I said, I would have no sons.

Previously it had been a tortuous journey over irrigation mounds and into pockets of soft sand but now we slid along a new road and soon an arm of the south jol, vividly remembered, came into view. It sits like a sphynx guarding the approaches to Seyuin, and now we were running past the large golden and white houses for which the wadi is famous. They rise behind high walls towards flat roofs and ornamental *rheims*. Made from the surrounding sand they appear to grow out of the ground and are topped by white-limed balustrades. Some windows with carved wooden shutters have splashes of white darting from the corners which were put there in troubled times so that the puff of white smoke from a gun could not be seen. The palms grow to a great height and send sharp shadows across the walls. Ahead we glimpsed white mosques and other houses, more ornate. Two camels led by an old man gazed with their usual air of disdain and a group of women in long saffron-coloured robes, vivid by contrast, made a scene of great beauty.

The centre of Seyuin lies at the opening of a side wadi and is a clutter of houses, walled cemetery, mosques, school, administration buildings and suk, all surrounding the Sultan's Palace. This huge building towers above the oasis and can be seen from every alleyway, *rheim* or roof. Its four towers, topped by ornate cupolas, are painted white and decorated in green, yellow and blue. An outer building or wall, incorporating a large and ornamental gateway, leads down wide steps to the village. The great solid structure is more like a fairy-tale palace and it contrasts with the lively, precarious scene of the suk below.

The little Kathiri Sultan lives in the palace during the winter and in the summer spends most of his time in a smaller palace in the gardens in the centre of the wadi.

The Adviser's offices are dilapidated now and the askari on guard rather lethargic. The familiar buzz of activity was increased slightly in the whirl of getting the Adviser and his family away on their yearly leave.

There is a new hospital, with an Indian and a brother of the Sultan as the two resident doctors, and electricity has been installed and is privately owned by a man who is fast becoming a millionaire. Near the suk a new public garden has been laid out with a small café, a row of dusty oleander bushes and an ugly cement pool with no water in it. A square and clinical looking building is the new rest house but I, being no V.I.P., was fortunately relegated to the old one which is a perfect example of traditional Hadhrami architecture. It is set, with the gardener's hut, in a large walled garden on the outskirts of the oasis and is therefore much cooler. Between the gardener's hut and the house is the well, shaded by palms with a deep ramp, used previously by the gardener and his donkey to pull the skin bucket to the surface, but now the creak of the wheel, the song, and the 'whoa!' of the gardener has been replaced by the chug-chug of the water pump's engine. As we drew up under the palms the caretaker, a lean old gentleman with a rather vain manner, greeted us.

Hadhramaut has the complacency of the much-loved and for generations Hadhrami men travelled to the East to make money, always to return to their valley. Reunited with their families – for their women would not travel – they enjoyed their wealth in leisure. One or two more children were born and as a diversion they built another beautiful house, palace or mosque. Often there was another wife who stayed in Indonesia and later on a son of that union accompanied his father back to Arabia, which accounts for the Polynesian caste of features so often found in this part of the world.

Why were these men so successful at business? Was there an especial quality similar perhaps to the Phoenicians? Or is it just that *all* people who take the initiative and leave their own countries make that extra effort? This idyllic state of affairs came to an end when the stringent new Indonesian currency regulations made it impossible for them to take their money out of these countries, and for a time the economy of the valley suffered badly. The halcyon days had gone but a more realistic prosperity is slowly taking its place, for with the Ingrams' Peace, tribe ceased to fight tribe and the settlers turned to the soil again. More land is being cultivated and irrigated and farmers are subsidized and encouraged to club together to buy machinery.

Harem Quarters

Despite the slowness of change, costs have risen here as elsewhere. Previously I could have bought a Hadhrami house for £500 and now it would cost about £5,000. The Rest House charged fifteen shillings per day for myself and Mubarak whilst previously I had hired the beautiful Beyt Bakrani for eighty shillings a month which included the services of the gardener to fill my water jars and the *jabia* (indoor swimming pool) and the dates from one palm tree.

Each morning Mubarak and I went to the market to buy the day's food. Beneath precariously erected awnings of matting were piles of tomatoes, onions, pumpkins, bananas, limes and oranges. In one corner was an open structure where freshly killed goat and the occasional sheep was quickly sold and we were always allowed the liver and kidneys. One enterprising lorry driver travelled overnight from the coast, bringing fresh fish. Three small arcades near by had tiny box-like shops where tinned goods, charcoal, grain, china and glass, cloth and all kinds of kitchen utensils could be bought. Deep in the old part of the oasis craftsmen still fashion fine gold and silver jewellery of traditional design. Some shop-owners remembered me. I was perhaps a little plumper, *el hamdu lillah!* Now, after all this time, I must surely speak excellent Arabic?

At the rest house I had been given the top or harem floor as befits a lone female. There were two bedrooms, three rheims and a bathroom with a large jar of water, an enamel basin on a stand and a drop lavatory. The lavatory is a slightly raised platform with a hole in the centre and a pocket at one side filled with a certain kind of soil used in place of toilet paper. Near by is a pail for swilling. The higher in the building one is, the better, for it is generally left to the dry air and the intense heat to dispose of the refuse below, and this is not always very successful; just as the use of European-style toilet paper can cause difficulties in a high wind.

Stairs led to the flat roof above, where in the late afternoon I sat on a mat watching the changing colours of the oasis. Rising high around the house was a deep sea of palms and the last rays of sun, shooting down the wadi towards us, turned the 'sphynx' cliff a fiery red. Odd noises, isolated in the stillness, floated up. Suddenly the electricity came on and the town sprang from the darkness. The light pierced the foliage and the house floated in an opaque sea of palm thongs. Time is lavish and wasteful here – as nature; and infinitely precious because of this.

Was I right to be so enamoured of this place? Should I have seen as others have, only the flies, the poverty, the bad sanitation and the indolence? They are certainly here, but the beauty outweighs it all; and nowhere was there the sterile unhappiness and loneliness so often encountered in our civilization.

The young British assistant adviser was seldom in Seyuin; with his guests he made trips to Tarim, Shibam and the northern areas, coming back only when a V.I.P. or the Commissioner was due for a lightning visit. The local men left in charge ran the place efficiently and without chaos in his absence. They insisted someone must be at hand to give me all the help and information I wanted and 'Ali' was produced.

Ali Asseggaff was a sayyid. He worked at the Adviserate and belonged to a large well-known Hadhrami family. He was a quietly spoken young man with finely drawn features and a gentleness of manner and movement typical of the idle sayyids. Recently married, he was very much in love and his pale bronze face and his expressive gestures were very pleasant to watch. Each afternoon he arrived at the rest house on a shining Vespa which he parked against one of the high palms, and was ready and willing to answer questions or accompany me in the Land-Rover on a jaunt. If we went by foot children followed and the crowd grew as we progressed. As he was a sayyid he had authority over them and the crowd was kept in check, but should I go alone or with Mubarak, chaos would ensue from which one or other of the elders would have to extricate me. This facet of the oasis life had not changed at all since my last visit, although the children must have seen many more Europeans during the intervening years.

Sayyid Ali was the ideal companion; it was immaterial to him what we did or how long we took in doing it. Everything was of interest and the day was not lost because nothing of note had been achieved. To keep to schedule was impossible for there was always somebody stopping to chat, or we could be given an invitation to tea.

There were journeys west to Wadi Do'an, a narrow and spectacular cut in the high jol, rich and green with palm groves. And in a side wadi behind the skyscraper Qaiti oasis of Shibam is the giant tomb of the Prophet Salih who, with his grandson Hud, is the patron saint of Hadhramaut. In some of the side wadis also one could find stunted bushes of incense, but nowhere the great forests of incense mentioned by Ptolemy, Hamdani and Pliny.

The most important person in the wadi is Sayyid Bubakr al Kaff, a one-time millionaire but not any longer because of his unbounded hospitality, generosity and the help he has given his own people in the wadi. The al Kaff sayyids live in Tarim but Sayyid Bubakr moved to Seyuin several years ago where he built two homes and a guest house; but now he was too old and ill to receive guests. It was shortly after this that he died.

We drove over to Tarim to have lunch with Josef al Kaff. It is the holy city of the wadi and famous as a seat of learning throughout southern Arabia. But learning produces new ideas and thoughts and there have been many troubled times within its walls. As we drove through the high gate of the oasis and past the unique cemetery with its myriads of headstones in pink, brown and white, I felt the same disquiet that I had experienced previously, for there is an oppressive air of fanaticism. Tarim has more spectacular buildings and palaces than either Seyuin or Shibam but the recent ones are garish and bizarre as well as being set at ungainly angles in the cluttered town. It is a smouldering, sullen town and tempers are never far from the surface. As a female, one feels very redundant.

The al Kaff hospital previously run by the Italian, Dr. Merucci, still functions but he is sorely missed. He now has his own practice in Jeddah.

'Please to go and see him, when you are in Jeddah,' they implored, 'and ask him to return.'

Josef al Kaff was much taller than the average Hadhrami and he has an energetic manner not often found in sayyids. One of their palaces is being turned into an hotel. It is a large ornate building with a fine swimming pool surrounded by a jungle of a garden, heady with the scent of roses and jasmine. There was an air of bustle for they were preparing for their first consignment of fifty American tourists. Josef studied the list, slightly bemused.

'They are all women!' he said, 'and they are all over sixty!'

We had lunch at his own house which is smaller, and the feeling of great affluence of previous times has gone. The al Kaff sayyids have been hosts to all travellers who come to Hadhramaut and whilst in Van der Meulen's time visitors were not so frequent, over the years they have increased and much of the family's fortune has gone in this way, for their hospitality was unbounded. As well as such people as Van der Meulen, Freya Stark and the Ingrams for whom it must have been a pleasure and privilege to entertain, there were complete strangers, many of whom could not even speak the language. Perhaps after all, fifty women, even if they were all over sixty, have one virtue – they would pay for their supper!

4

Open Sesame

The tree doth not withdraw its shade, even from the
woodcutter.   — HITOPADESA

NO ONE but myself believed the journey north would be
possible; that permission would be given. With my usual
mental stubbornness I had never visualized anything else. But
I did experience a shock, with excitement perhaps, as I read:

Received Jeddah today approval to pass overland. However,
you cannot go before itinerary has been approved by
authorities. Please send me urgently proposed date of com-
mencement of journey and detailed itinerary of route in
order this may be telegraphed to Jeddah as soon as possible.
Pughe.

'So now you can go,' said Ali, his untroubled face registering
no emotion; if he thought the whole project unusual or precarious he never showed it, and I felt he would set about sending me to the moon with exactly the same *savoir faire*.
'Yes,' I answered, 'when I know which way I *am* going, and
Jeddah approves the route.'
It was necessary to decide my date of departure immediately
and to work out an itinerary that would be feasible and satisfy
the Saudis. I had been told to keep out of the Yemen at all
costs and especially out of Republican hands for once having
made contact with them I could not pass into Saudi Arabian
territory. Also what kind of propaganda would be made of it
should they capture me? With the continuous advance and
retreat of both the Royalist and Republican armies, was it
possible to know how far the Royalists had been pushed back
towards the desert?

47

'I shall have to stay far to the east and as near the desert as possible,' I said to Ali.

'I have a friend,' he said, 'who is an agent. He will know the best way for you to go.'

'What kind of agent?'

'He arranges lorries taking pilgrims to Mecca for the Hajj.'

Many of the pilgrim lorries were already assembling in the wadi near the hospital. They park here whilst the pilgrims are inoculated and procure permits to travel to Mecca. There were huge brightly painted vehicles, Mercedes Benz, Leyland, International and Volvo, all with extra high sides to take the large quota of humans.

We drove into town in the early evening to meet the agent. The last shaft of light shot down the valley towards us and tiny birds, flying in a scatter ahead of the vehicle, had wings so thin and transparent that the light filtered through, turning them into ethereal ghost-like creatures.

The agent was not as gentle as Ali and far more worldly, he wore European clothes and regarded me with a calculating eye. Two other men with the same air of sophistication were introduced as the owner of the lorry and his driver.

'I have asked them to tell you the best route to the Saudi border,' said the agent, 'but they will expect some money for the information.'

Ali was shocked.

'It is all right,' I said, 'so long as they give the correct route.' It was however an unfortunate start, for once it became established that I pay for every piece of information and help, I may have to bribe all along the route. But wasn't it, after all, an age-old custom? And didn't the precious incense cost six hundred per cent its original price by the time it arrived in Damascus because of the bribes and dues taken all along the line? I was no precious cargo, but customs die hard.

We were standing near the palace gates and had drawn the usual crowd of small boys.

'Come,' said Ali, glancing at the upturned faces, 'it is better everyone does not know of your plans.'

48

A Route Through the Yemen

We drove down a side wadi and stopped where it was quite isolated and dark. Our passengers in the back of the Land-Rover were having a heated argument.

'What is the matter?' I asked Ali.

'They want fifty shillings before they will tell you the best route,' he said in a resigned voice.

I turned out my pockets. 'Fifteen shillings is all I have with me,' I said.

'Give it to me.' He passed it over to the owner of the lorry who took it without further remark or demur.

There are two tracks possible during war-time: one goes far to the east into the Rub el Khali and is very difficult and isolated, whilst the other follows the base of the high Yemen massif and is much nearer the fighting zones. The latter is used by the pilgrim lorries who are not likely to be bombed, except by mistake.

'Ask them, Ali,' I said, 'to give me the actual names of the towns on the pilgrim route.'

'There are no towns, all they can give are the names of sand dunes, wells, hills and wadis,' he said.

'That is better than nothing. I must have something to send the Saudis.'

With much argument and supposition as to my capabilities in driving the Land-Rover across the desert, the list was compiled. 'The route runs north to Husn al Abr, the desert post lying at the approaches to Wadi Hadhramaut; north-west across the lower reaches of the Rub el Khali through the Raiyan sands to the old well of Mushairiqa; through Wadi Hubail; around Jebel Hureita; across Wadi Knabb and Wadi Itema to the sands of Tayib el Ism . . .'

'The Sitt will not be able to cross Tayib el Ism,' said the driver of the lorry.

'She has crossed Sudan (the Sahara) many times. She has come from Kuwait to Jeddah alone,' said Ali scornfully.

'Wallah!' said the driver.

'And after the sands of Tayib el Ism?' I asked, wishing to have my fifteen shillings worth.

The driver glanced at me, regarding my face for the first time. There is an affinity between drivers who take vehicles on

rough journeys and now, suddenly, we two were working out
the route together.

'After the sands of Tayib el Ism,' he said, 'is Jebel Ajashir,
and on to Khadhra Well in Wadi Najran which is Saudi,'
he said. '*Helas.*'

'*Helas,*' I confirmed.

Then in the way of men the world over, he repeated the
instructions from beginning to end.

'From Husn al Abr,' he said, 'you go to Raiyan Sands where
there are mountains and sand and a well, a very old well . . .'

'Mushairiqa?'

He nodded. 'Later there is Wadi Hubail with more sand
and Ghas, where you must go between two mountains on the
horizon ahead. After Ghas there are the high sand dunes of el
Hureita; slowly, slowly here because of bombs. Then Sugal
Gora which is more sand . . .'

'It is nothing but a series of sand dunes,' I said to Ali. 'Are
you sure this is correct?'

The lorry driver nudged my arm and continued: 'In the
hills to Wadi Knabb where you will see bedu for the first time –
and bombs.'

'Tch,' I said, rather ineffectually.

'And afterwards – Tayib el Ism with very bad sands, very bad,'
he repeated. '*In sha allah* you pass Tayib el Ism, there is Jebel
Ajashir where there are three mountains. Pass two of them on
your left, and go between third. Afterwards and a long way
round; but not difficult if you do not get lost, is the well of
Khudra. Soon, then, you are in Najran. *El hamdu lillah!*'

'Oh, it is simple,' I said to Ali, 'all I need are sand channels
and a bucket of water!'

'It is not good to joke,' he said, looking a little disturbed.

I hoped he had not noticed the remarks about the bombs, for
it was obvious I was going through Yemeni territory, and
fighting territory at that.

'Ali,' I said quietly, 'I have come so far to take the journey.
In the Sahara they say I am an *efrita* and that the desert looks
after me.'

'*Impkin,*' he said, inscrutable as ever.

I thanked them all and turned on the Land-Rover's headlights, which revealed a sea of small faces, for the children had followed us down. My journey was a secret no longer.

A signal was dispatched to Aden giving my route and the proposed date of departure – April the First. The fate of the whole journey rested on Jeddah's approval. There had been great surprise in many quarters that the application had not been turned down immediately. Some thought it was mere diplomacy and that refusal of the submitted route would be received in due course. Others wondered if after all, I did not have 'friends at court'. I began to wonder myself.

Mubarak was becoming restless. He had procured a pilgrim passport to accompany me to Saudi Arabia and he could not believe that a *nasrani* must wait for permission to go anywhere. He felt I was obviously intending to potter around the wadis for months as I had done on my previous visit.

'You wish to go back to Mukalla?' I asked him.

'You do not go to Najran and Jeddah?' he asked.

'Yes, Mubarak, but I must wait for permission,' he regarded me passively, 'this is true, Mubarak. It is not easy for a *nasrani* to go to Saudi Arabia.'

When rumours came up from Mukalla that his wife had taken their small son away from the town, he announced his intention of returning there, and laden with his blanket now filled with several belongings, he boarded a lorry making the overnight journey to the coast.

The activity in the wadi near the hospital was abating, for many of the pilgrim lorries had already departed for Mecca; the long pilgrimage had begun. The religion of Islam should not be so alien to us for it includes much that is known in the Old and New Testament. God has another name, but Mahammad was God's messenger just as Jesus and Abraham were before him. Perhaps it is the public and independent ritual of prayer that makes it appear so different, but the constant companionship of Allah is enviable. Now at this period, thousands of Moslems were moving towards the Holy City; the direction in which I hoped to go.

At last it arrived – the signal I had been waiting for: 'Permission granted to travel overland to Jeddah permit following. Pughe.'

Open Sesame

The Saudis had agreed! With the permit was a letter reminding me to keep away from Yemen territory and advising that I would probably be met at the Saudi Arabian border and escorted north.

With the arrival of summer the desert is 'closed' to vehicles, for the intense heat plays havoc with engines and the crossing is therefore much more dangerous at this time. Also bandits become active for there would be no protection for a vehicle venturing alone. At the Government workshop where the Land-Rover was being overhauled, I sought out the head mechanic Hussain who had practical knowledge of many of the desert routes.

'How can I leave Husn al Abr if the desert is closed?' I asked.

'The lorry drivers *say* they are going to Attik which is south-west, but once out of sight of the fort at al Abr, they turn north.' He said, 'That is what you will have to do!'

'She would be stopped at the first check-post and sent back – or interned,' said a little man, raising his head from a large ledger.

'What do you mean, "Interned"?' I asked.

'They are Yemeni check-posts, most of them.'

The less said about that the better, I felt.

'The only way,' said Hussain, 'is for you to travel with one of the pilgrim lorries. You would not be so conspicuous.'

'Would they take me, a *nasrani*?'

They considered this.

'And a woman at that!'

'It is your only chance of getting through.'

There would be a certain anonymity about following the pilgrims and at the check-posts the overworked officials would have less time to concentrate on me.

'We know the man who will tell you,' said Hussain at last. 'I shall send a boy for him.'

'Who is he and why should he know?'

'He owns one of the lorries and he often goes himself.'

It was some time before a slight man in his early thirties came slowly across the yard. Everything about Aytha Balfass was unhurried and quiet, even his voice. He looked taller than he was, as most Hadhramis do, for they are slim and well proportioned. He had delicate expressive hands and it seemed incredible that he was going to drive one of the huge lorries over the rough terrain. But he became an endless source of surprises in the weeks that followed, for he never raised his voice even in the most desperate circumstances, had authority and the loyalty of everyone in the convoy. He confirmed I could travel with his two lorries.

'And what will it cost?' I asked.

'If the sitt will pay a fee to the guide who comes with us to Wadi Knabb,' he said, 'one hundred shillings.'

I readily agreed. 'Except for the guide's fee, what other expenses will there be?' I asked.

He considered for a second. 'You may have to pay an extra one hundred shillings to enter Saudi Arabia at Najran,' he said, 'as the pilgrims do.'

'As the pilgrims do!' I was enchanted.

His lorries were leaving the next morning for Ghoutha, which is half-way to Husn al Abr. Their progress would be slow for they stop many times to pick up pilgrims. I could follow later. Aytha stood up as though everything was settled.

'Thank you,' I said as we shook hands. He smiled and went quietly off across the yard.

It is always the same! The important deciding factors that make such a journey possible are simple and easy; they fall into place with little outside effort; if it is right it will happen – *in sha Allah*.

But how would the pilgrims react to having a *nasrani* with them on this the great religious pilgrimage of their life? Tolerance towards the disbeliever was never preached in Moslem law; would they be resentful of the intrusion? I must try and be as self-contained as possible and so set about looking for a boy to accompany me.

The Adviser's chauffeur who was on leave during his boss's absence wanted to make the pilgrimage.

'He will be grateful for the lift,' said Ali, 'it will save him money and be more comfortable than in one of the crowded lorries.'

The chauffeur Hassan was taller and tougher looking than most Hadhramis. He had a calculating eye and a mottled skin.

Open Sesame

'You would like to come in the Land-Rover?' I asked.

'Yes, memsahib. Thank you, memsahib,' he said.

'Well, if you care to do the things Mubarak did, I shall pay you as well.'

'How much?' He was very quick.

'The same as I paid Mubarak; ten shillings a day. *Tamam?*'

'*Tamam,*' he agreed.

After each lap of a journey there are renewed preparations; my calico bags were refilled with tea, sugar, flour and rice and some biscuits and tinned goods bought in the suk. Hassan found two gerbas (goatskins) which would hold three and a half gallons each, but now that I was travelling in convoy my water capacity was not so vital. I had one jerrycan, two gerbas, two two-gallon plastic cans and another one-gallon one. Sixteen or seventeen gallons in all.

The most important thing was to know the mileage so that I could work out the amount of petrol needed for the entire journey to the Saudi Arabian border at Najran. Finding the exact mileage of a journey is almost impossible. No Arab knows distances, other than by the *time* it takes to go from one place to another, and this applies to lorry drivers as well. To add to the confusion they will tell you what they think you wish to hear. 'It is so many hours from here to there. But there are dunes – you might have to go a whole day out of your way to miss them. But kilometres?' They will put their right hand under their left elbow. 'It is surely that far!'

The distances ranged from six hundred to eleven hundred kilometres. Finally I bought another two jerrycans which made eleven altogether. With my extra petrol tank I now had a capacity of just over sixty gallons.

The evening before we were to leave, Hassan demanded three times more money from me. 'I shall have to do so much,' he said, 'cook, and when the Land-Rover breaks down, mend it.'

'You were coming for nothing, originally,' I said.

'I do everything, I drive . . .'

'Oh no, you do not drive!' I said.

'Also, I want one hundred shillings for the pilgrim fee.'

It was too late to find another boy. 'This is a disgrace,'

A Pistol at My Head

I said to the British assistant who was back in Seyuin. 'This driver is putting a pistol at my head.'

'You know what they are,' he said, shrugging.

'I do not. It has never happened to me before.'

He looked inadequate, so I compromised by paying a lump sum which was double the original amount and agreeing to pay the pilgrim fee if it should be necessary. It is a national sport to score off British officials and servants previously employed by them are better avoided. I sighed for my honest, diligent Mubarak.

5

Towards the Yemen

Meglio solo che mal accompagnato.
    – ITALIAN PROVERB

THEY were threshing in the wadi as we drove west. The
women, trailing black gowns and wearing peaked witches' hats
of straw, stood in pools of yellow, beating the grain. Others
fed the grain as a camel or donkey moved endlessly and
leisurely in a circle. Nearer Shibam we passed back into
Qaiti territory and a more advanced peasant drove a Land-
Rover round and round pulling a thick palm trunk over the
ground.

The 'skyscrapers' of Shibam rose out of the centre of the wadi
ahead, spectacular as ever, though the whole scene is now
slightly smudged with the scatter of old oil drums, burst tyres
and broken lorries that lie around in the wadi below the city
gates. But the women in gowns of cobalt blue still move through
the great gateway and make their way to the well in the wadi
bed, the brilliant colour of their clothes setting off to perfection
the towering buildings and high palms.

Beyond the oasis the new granite road continues west so that
in a few hours one can traverse the whole main part of the wadi.
Not so long ago the journey taken by donkey or in one of the
few vehicles brought in pieces from the coast and reassembled
in the wadi, could take days. To approach an oasis slowly, to
stop and rest one's animals, makes for an infinitely more
pleasant journey, but to proceed in such a way today, with
vehicles whizzing past, would not only be uncomfortable, but
kinky.

We stopped at Gatn and filled all our containers with petrol
for being back in Qaiti territory there is no double duty. The
Sultans of Gatn owned the best library in the wadi and similar

to the al Kaff Sayyids are noted for their hospitality. The present Sultan is an intelligent young man who works in the Administration in Aden and his large palace which over-shadows the small oasis was closed and deserted. We continued along the base of the south cliff and stopped to make tea under one of the large elb trees that grow out of the sand in the wadi bed. The elb plays a great part in the life of the people; the Arabs say it is a tree in the seventh heaven with its roots in the sixth and from its spiked branches Christ's crown of thorns was made. The timber is used for the pillars and shutters of houses and above all its spreading branches make a fine spot for camping. Now the dom fruit, the small red and orange berries were ripening. They are rather tasteless, but neverthe-less eaten with relish by the locals.

By late morning we had already arrived at the confluence of the three wadis where Do'an, al Aiser and the wide approaches of Hadhramaut meet. It is safer though longer to hug the cliffs but we cut across the centre of the wadi and were soon in a jumble of dunes, ridges and soft sand. Suddenly, we came upon an old Land-Rover stuck fast in the sand. Beside it was a young man and all around was churned-up ground and broken branches where he had been trying to extricate the vehicle, for he had no sand channels of any kind. We turned the Land-Rover and drove towards him. He carried no water and had been stranded here since early morning. With the help of my own sand channels we managed to transfer the old vehicle on to firm ground in less than fifteen minutes and gave the young man some water, making sure he drank it slowly, then watched him disappear over the bumpy ground.

Into this area came the Yafa'i, the forerunners of the present Qaiti dynasty, four hundred years ago. In their own mountains to the west is the Holy City of al Qara, the High Place which is set spectacularly on top of a bare mountain. Their lineage descends directly from holy families of Priest-Chiefs who led the worship of tribal gods before Islam. Even today they serve two gods in al Qara: Allah in the mosque and Yafa the god who inhabits the holy drum of the tribe.

A long low dune, well remembered, lay ahead of us, for on the previous journey my Land-Rover had stuck badly in the soft sand. But now with the higher powered vehicle, or my added experience, we sailed over, topping it easily to see ahead the village of Ghoutha which lay at the foot of the west cliff. To the north of the village was the police fort and a new building – a modern caravanserai – stood near by. It was painted white and decorated in blue and of the worst nouveau-Hadhrami style. Was this the fate awaiting the beautiful countryside should oil and the resulting prosperity come to the land?

They gave us tea in the guardroom where guns and jackets hung on the wall and several grey blankets, neatly rolled, lay against the walls. A small charcoal burner with teapot and tiny cups made a focal point of the room which smelt of smoke and leather.

Aytha and the lorries had not arrived and the askari in charge suggested we continue to Husn al Abr where there was an Adviser and a guest room. However, until the day was cooler they gave me a room in which to rest; it looked north along the pilgrim track where, despite the hard stony surface, indentations of lorries that had passed that way could be seen. At this spot the tracks from many wadis merged but only one lay ahead, leading north towards Mecca and all who passed along it were Moslems – all except me.

When it was cooler we set off with a soldier – for protection – and an old man of the Nahd tribe who lived along the wadi. He climbed into the back of the vehicle groaning and limping badly but calling down the blessings of Allah on my head.

Here the desert and the northern jol merge with the valleys of the more settled inhabitants. To our left stretched difficult dunes of the Ramlet Sabatain which form a barrier to Shabwa, Ayadh and Beihan.

As we drove on Thukmain, the two pinnacles standing at the entrance to Wadi Ser came into view. They are a distinctive landmark for travellers and can be seen for miles around. The shallow wadi had bushes of acacia, green alba and ra and along its base are many wells. After we had covered fifteen miles the old man signalled me to stop and climbing out set off in a sprightly manner towards a cluster of umbrella acacias, his limp miraculously cured.

The Nahd tribe which are now half nomad and half settled,

claim a large area from Qatn in the east to Ramlet Sabatain in the west and to the northern edges of the desert. The tribe is believed to have originally come from the Yemen and they have preserved in writing all the bedouin laws and customs of Hadhramaut through the ages. The Hakm of the Al bin Ajaj of Ghoutha was for centuries the final appeal judge for all the tribes as far as the eastern approaches to Hadhramaut; he was consulted by chiefs settling difficult cases and even today with the establishment of courts, this practice continues.

We climbed with difficulty from the wadi to a rocky escarpment, bumping across it until finally a sharp upward turn brought us broadside on to Wadi al Abr. The wells of the wadi lay in the sandy bed and on the far bank was a picturesque fort with a cluster of new buildings near by. Husn al Abr is the entrance to Hadhramaut and its wells are as old as they are important, for the abundant water supplies caravans going to the Yemen and Saudi Arabia as well as to Shabwa, Attik and Beihan. Previously there had been the fort and a few black tents, now it was a community with a sizeable contingent, the Adviser's bungalow, a mechanic's shop and living quarters, two buildings for the medical officer and others for the police and pilgrim personnel. Beyond a high dune was a settlement of black tents, swelled at the moment, for the bedouin gather to sell to the pilgrims and the price of goats had almost doubled.

The Hadhrami Adviser was away in the desert but some soldiers, the medical officer, the mechanic and several small boys welcomed us. There were many of the Sei'ar tribe, dressed simply in a futah with an elegant jambia stuck in a belt. A good jambia is difficult to buy now and can cost as much as £65. The Sei'ar were known as 'The Wolves of the Desert' and they gave Ingrams a great deal of trouble. They were successful raiders living on the fringe of the desert and along the plateau of Reidat el Sei'ar, carrying out raids from Wadi al Abr to the territories of the Mahra and the Manahil when it was a simple matter to disappear into the desert again. They had few friends and travelled mostly by night except when they visited Shibam, for they had a truce with that town and bought charcoal and saf for mat-making to sell in the suk. Pliny says they were descended from Kinda and they practise the old

custom of trial marriages of two-month duration, after which
there is either a marriage or the girl goes back to her family.
They look deceptively gentle with soft curly hair and quiet
engaging manners as they advance to shake hands, which
they do by placing palm against palm and bending forward
until the tips of their noses meet, when they give an odd kissing
sound, perhaps more like a catch in the breath. From what
dawn of time does this custom originate, for surely it derives
from the searching use of the Third Eye.

The guest room at the Adviser's bungalow was at the end of
a long veranda and it overlooked the wadi. It contained a large
metal wardrobe, a tin table and a metal door that did not
fasten.

Most of Hassan's energies went in trying to find people to do
his work for him. The gardener had been enrolled to load the
Land-Rover in Seyuin and small boys enlisted at Qatn to move
the jerrycans about; all of whom had to be tipped. He now
commandeered the Adviser's boy, a smiling child of twelve
and instructed him to prepare food. I should have been firmer
from the start but the unaccustomed pain in my back had left
me impatient, lacking in judgement and unable to view the
situation dispassionately. Not for me the stoicism, the spiritual
uplift of this new experience – realization through suffering. I
was gaining a healthy respect for those travellers, stricken by
pain and illness who continue with their usual erudite percep-
tion, curiosity and above all good humour. My disability had
left me with a numbed brain and senses that were fast becoming
a barrier between me and my companions. Worst of all,
Hassan was getting on my nerves, was sapping my sense of
humour; and a journey without that wasn't worth making.

'Memsahib?'

It was almost a whisper. I raised my head from the camp bed.
Abdullah, the boy, was standing in the doorway with a huge
pot of tea.

'Memsahib. Inglese – tea.' He put the pot down on the floor
beside the bed, giving me a big slow grin.

The bedouin encampment of black tents was a friendly place
where there was always a welcome to share what little they had.

Bedu Hospitality

A small kid's skin full of camel's milk hung near the entrance to some of the tents and anyone passing helped themselves. A young sheikh of the Nahd took me to a tent which was set over a frame shaped like a half walnut shell. Our host, a gaunt middle-aged man with a young wife, served coffee made from the husks of the bean. The wife, in a limp black gown wore no jewellery except for one solid silver bangle. Her small son hid himself behind her, but finally curiosity overcame him and he staggered across the sand and dropped in my lap. But the mother was wary. I was, after all, a *nasrani*. She tried to coax the child away but he would have none of it.

'Your silver bracelet,' I said, to distract her, 'it is very lovely.'

Immediately she took it off and handed it over, implying that I keep it, but I passed it back. She had been prepared, as custom and the law of hospitality demand, to give away her one piece of jewellery.

I went often to the tents, for the way of life is a natural reaction against all that we know today. Here the moment was all that mattered, the future could not be greatly changed by effort and the past was no longer regretted. It is the simplicity that draws one, even if only for a time; the wells give water, the animals milk and although nature is hard, it is, with Allah, their constant companion. My hosts accepted with pleasure but without thanks the sugar and tea I brought and the children, quite without prompting from their parents, immediately shared the sweets with their companions. The conversation sometimes had a familiar ring; goats cost more, the young men looked towards the oil fields in the east; but finally there were the timeless tales of wadis and old wells across the country, names mentioned by Pliny and Strabo and our Bible.

'And the old route north?' I asked.

'The old one went along this wadi and on to the Ayabed wells, but as the lorries travel faster they go direct to the wells of Mushairiqa which they can reach in less than a day.'

'Wadi Ayabed becomes very narrow near the wells,' said the young Sheikh, 'and there are carvings on the rocks.'

Here again there was obviously a narrow defile which had been used as a check-point on the route.

'Is it possible to go there?'

'Of course. Ahmed will arrange it.'

'Ahmed?'

'The Adviser; he will be back this evening.'

He was, in fact, waiting on the veranda when we returned to the house, a good-looking young man with a sense of humour, and a quiet air of authority who spoke excellent English. Yes, I could go to Wadi Ayabed and he would arrange for a guide to take me in the morning. I was beginning to have a healthy respect for the cool efficiency of the official Hadhrami.

It was barely seven o'clock the next morning when a little man of the Sei'ar tribe arrived at the veranda steps. He had a round leathery face and tilted his head to one side, his lips were drawn back slightly and his eyes permanently half closed in the way of the desert bedu. The tiny frame was covered in a long shirt, tightly belted, which gave him a 'little girl' look.

'But I know you!' I said. He had been employed by the Locust Control geologists to guard supplies of petrol left in the area and to report on the movements of locusts. Yes, of course he remembered me and it seemed quite natural that I should be here again. But where were the sahibs?

'They are both in England,' I said, 'both are married – and with sons.'

'*El hamdu lillah!* I will take you – just the same.'

It is difficult to judge the distance to Wadi Ayabed for the terrain is difficult for a vehicle and several times we were forced to retrace our steps. After driving roughly north-north-west for an hour, a shallow wadi began to form which finally narrowed to a cut in the rock now half filled with sand. We left the Land-Rover and struggled over the soft ground. It was a natural defile no more than fifteen feet across with many Qatabanian and Minean inscriptions as well as some water signs. We scooped the sand away and found drawings of hands and the tops of two wells that were completely sanded up. Amongst the finer inscriptions were later scratchings made by passing travellers giving, no doubt, information on the route ahead and there were more recent efforts still, one of which read: *Mhb srm Ism* (Sharam copulated with Ilsam).

'The Sei'ar are Everywhere'

'What territory is this? Who lives around here?' I asked.

'Lives?' my companion looked nonplussed.

'Do the Sei'ar graze here?'

'Of course,' with a wide sweep of the hand, 'the Sei'ar are everywhere. And the Karab and sometimes even the Manahil.'

To the bedouin there are no borders and they go wherever there is grazing and water. Or in the old days, plunder. Many deny they owe allegiance to anyone but their own sheikh, and others even though they spend most of their time in the confines of Hadhramaut, call themselves Saudi or Yemeni. A sheikh of the Dahmi tribe in the north, on the orders of Faisal ibn Saud, set up a series of cairns running north-north-west from al Abr and through this defile, to open up the ancient route; and this same sheikh collected taxes for flocks on behalf of the Wahhabi sultan as far south as the Abr Wells.

As we moved along the narrow passage the sand became softer and deeper; one day it will be completely buried and its location forgotten. How many other passes and caravan posts lie beneath the sand with carvings and inscriptions which could answer many of the questions still asked about Arabia's past?

We returned to the Land-Rover and drove north-west again until we met the tracks going direct from Husn al Abr to the wells of Mushairiqa which is the next watering place on the old route.

'We can go back now,' I said to the Sei'ar, 'for later I go direct from Husn al Abr to Mushairiqa.'

'Where you go?'

'I am with the pilgrims.'

'*Wallah sah!*' he regarded me with interest.

'Well, not to Mecca, I must go round the Holy City.'

'But you come back?'

I nodded. 'Some time. Then I shall cross the Rub el Khali,' I said, 'I shall cross the Sands.'

'Good,' he said. 'I shall be here.'

*   *   *

In the late afternoon Abdullah the boy came running along the veranda. He burst into my room.

Towards the Yemen

'Aytha!' he cried excitedly.

I followed him out on to the veranda and he pointed across the wadi. I could see nothing, but a few seconds later my eye caught two tiny specks moving along the black ridge. They crawled with the stolid slowness of vehicles loaded far beyond their capacity. As we watched they dipped out of sight and in a short time reappeared on the far bank. Now they moved towards us and plunged into the soft sand, coming steadily nearer like two colourful overfed toads.

My companions of the weeks to follow were piled to dizzy heights on top of the oil drums, boxes and their own bundles. The sides of the lorries bulged with sacks of grain and rows of water skins. With a mighty effort the vehicles climbed the near bank, chugged finally on to harder ground and came to rest beside the customs shed.

Immediately the vehicles stopped, the silhouettes began to disintegrate; the great mass moved, as pilgrim after pilgrim disengaged himself and climbed down. The outlines as we watched diminished slowly and there seemed no end to the people the lorries could disgorge. The pilgrims were dressed in a varied assortment of clothes and each carried a plastic container or water skin as they turned swiftly towards the wells. At last the lorries stood denuded and strangely inert. On the body of the lorry, a platform and wooden sides had been built making it possible to take two rows of people. Those who sat in the base of the lorry saw nothing of the journey but were protected from the sun and the cold; whilst above them was a solid mass of people sitting and standing. The lorries carried between ninety and a hundred people each and the passengers paid one hundred shillings for the journey as well as another hundred shillings at the Saudi Arabian border as pilgrim fees. They brought their own food and were allowed few clothes except the ones they wore and the *ihram* clothes for the final entrance into Mecca. The Saudis allows each pilgrim to import two rugs which they can sell to allay the cost of the journey.

Aytha, calm and unruffled, had replaced his decorative futah for a long white dishdasher and a short European-style jacket of black cloth. A red and white kuffiyah framed his face and showed a ring of loose black curls. With a good sense of

Friends Amongst the Karab Tribe

diplomacy he took me amongst the pilgrims, as the first appearance being with him would make things easier for me. He never remarked on the reason for such things, he just did them. Even in Seyuin he had omitted to mention that we would come to several check-posts in Yemen territory and may pass through mined and dangerous areas. He sensed that whilst I probably knew about these things they were better left unsaid. An unspoken understanding grew between us which made it possible for me to know just when to efface myself or when my appearance would cause no embarrassment.

I had expected there would be a more sanctified atmosphere about the pilgrimage even at the start of the journey; but there was a cheerful festive air as though despite the hardships ahead, a happy holiday was contemplated.

We were to leave in the late afternoon. But which afternoon? It was impossible to think of any kind of schedule and impatience and haste are viewed with suspicion. There were over two hundred pilgrims to be checked and progress would be slow; one day here or there was not important. There can be no greater nightmare than to travel with Arabs if one is in a hurry!

The wells of al Abr were the focal point and a scene of constant activity. Previously there were forty in the wadi and the four remaining ones have concrete surrounds which makes it easier for the bedouin to pull their water. Unhappily the picturesque goatskins are being replaced by sections of the lorries' discarded inner tubes which are sealed at one end and filled from the other. They lie around on the sand tight with water, like black monsters; more practical perhaps but far less attractive. Occasionally a couple of camels with a family arrived up the wadi and camped near the wells. One family of the Karab tribe arrived in the evening. There were two wives. The first one, Fatma, was probably about thirty, she was slim and strong with large eyes, withdrawn but tolerant. The other, a recent bride, looked about fifteen years old. She was vivacious, pleased with her new status but liable to wander off and frolic like a child. The husband was middle-aged and quiet. Mahammad decreed that a man must treat all his wives with equal consideration. But what man can fool a woman when it comes to his preference? It must however be easier to accept a husband's new wife when it is the law, than it would be for us to accept our husband's mistress. The Karab family 'adopted' me and every time I walked towards the well, others would point to them accepting their claim on me. Fatma pulled the bucket up from the well's depths with strong easy movements and she worked at great speed. Once at the top she would pause to chat. They were going north.

'Do you go right across – towards Riyadh?' I asked.

She nodded. 'Sometimes,' she said, 'the women go.'

'Women – alone?'

'Yes. It is good.'

'Will you take me?'

She laughed, assenting. 'The next rains!' she promised, and calling the new wife, she handed her the skin bucket and we went off to guide the camels back to their possessions.

The child-wife, having taken the bucket, worked as best she could; but she was small and less accustomed to the heavy weight. In the hubbub of men, women, children and camels her efforts went unnoticed by all; all except for her husband who came quietly over and taking the taut rope continued to heave the bucket up for her.

The mechanics' Nissen hut had two beds along the sides of the wall, a couple of boxes and the familiar smell of oil and petrol. The mechanics treated me with more friendliness than they would a *nasrani* man, they gave me tea and talked end-lessly of engines, breakdowns and bad sand dunes. If they found it unusual that I knew the difference between a petrol pump and a distributor, they did not show it. The Land-Rover, however, commanded their unbounded admiration. Lorries became stuck, broke down, blew up, but the Land-Rover sailed over everything. The Land-Rover, they assured me, was the 'Gazelle of the Desert'.

Here, as at Ayadh there were rumours of the presence of oil. The boys had many theories, for it is the treasure search of the twentieth century. They showed me pieces of petrified wood which, in their opinion, was a clue to the presence of oil. Its non-discovery to date is a sore point with all southern Arabians and the usual rumours circulate. I have heard them in many countries during early explorations and before the first big strike; and they always follow the same pattern: i.e. that the British have found oil but will not admit it; are suppressing it; or are already pumping it out secretly! Others go even a little further and say the British do not wish it to be found because a country once wealthy from oil is too great a responsibility. In the meantime millions are being spent in the search and the oil men, conditioned to these reactions, press on regardless.

There was an air of excitement and anticipation amongst the pilgrims, for word had gone round that we should congregate at the passport office. Now they were dressed in their poorest clothes for the long, dusty journey north and the women stood apart, heavily veiled and in long black clothes. The activity was perpetual as the figures climbed up and down from the lorries and bags of grain and goatskins were fixed to the sides. They glanced curiously at the Land-Rover and everything I did was watched with interest.

This year coincided with Dhu-al-Hajja in the year A.H. 1384. We were nearing the end of the Islamic year which is the time to perform the Hajj to Mecca. Previously it was considered necessary to make the pilgrimage by foot and the more difficult the journey the greater the reward in after-life. Many pilgrims took twelve to fifteen years to complete the journey, often marrying and having children *en route*. Now that time is the essence, they make the whole trip by lorry, aeroplane or by ship, and over one million people enter Mecca each year. Jeddah on the Red Sea is the main sea and air port for Mecca and during the preceding days planes arrive every ten minutes and the harbour is crowded with pilgrim ships.

The simplicity of the Moslem religion is its strength for it was nurtured in the harsh life of the desert. It stands steadfast in the essential oneness of God. All that is demanded is to pray five times a day kneeling and facing Mecca; to praise God; and to fast during the month of Rhamadan. It is forbidden to eat pork or ham, drink alcohol or to smoke. Everyone should make the Hajj if possible, and give alms. Many Moslems give ten per cent of their income to the poor, though with increasing taxation this will probably decline. On the less frugal side a Moslem is allowed four wives at a time and he may have concubines. On average there are seldom more than two wives and this is governed by economics – and fashion, for it is considered more advanced to have only one wife these days. In isolated desert places a second wife is company for the other woman and this applies definitely to the upper classes when the wives are in purdah. Many of these women live amicably together and take as much interest in each other's children as in their own.

Such is the creed and customs of Islam followed today by untold millions. It owed its inception to Mahammad who was born in Mecca in A.D. 570 and was quite illiterate. When he grew up he became a successful desert trader, and was already forty when he had a vision and the Angel Gabriel revealed to him that there was but one God. At first when he tried to spread this doctrine he met with great opposition in Mecca where pilgrims came to worship at the shrines of over three hundred and fifty deities. After twelve years he was forced to leave the city and made the journey north to Medina; almost immediately he met with more success and soon his doctrine became religious law. He made several journeys but died at the age of sixty-two. After his death his revelations and teachings, incorporated with a great amount of desert lore, were collected into the Koran. There are many similarities with the old and new Testaments, and Moslems believe that Jesus was a prophet but not that he was God's son; though Mahammad accepted Jesus' virgin birth and ascension as fact.

In the extraordinarily short time during his life and within ten years of his flight to Medina, Islamic law was established in his country and spread rapidly so that by medieval times it had extended from India to Spain, bringing with it a new civilization in science and the arts. Once it was firmly established, the religion took on a less operative approach, and a gradual decline and withdrawal from the outside, non-Moslem world set in. There is something in the essence of Islam that does not lend itself to an offensive or operative control. The coming of oil and its accompanying wealth has given many Moslem countries a new awareness, but it has brought problems also. Islam may survive because of its simplicity; but just as the Arabic language must find words for the new things that have come into their lives from the west, so they must adjust their religious beliefs and laws to the twentieth century. Many of them are already lax in carrying out old laws, but the great majority of the 600 to 700 million Moslems in the world today do still regard their religion as part of everyday life, not just a one day a week reminder as so many Christians do.

Now the lorries were almost full, the last straggler had been called and the vehicles stood low in the sand. I wandered down to have a last look at the wells and Fatma was tying the final bundle on to the second camel.

'Good-bye, Fatma,' I said, 'do not forget, Riyadh!'

She turned, her fine eyes softening with amusement, 'After the rains – I come!' she called. Then there was a 'Hip!' and a 'Whoa!' The animal rose. With a last slap on its rump, the little procession moved off; the man first, the girl-wife and Fatma bringing up the rear. Perhaps she will be there waiting, after the rains.

6

Live Now — Die Later

Hate is just a failure of the imagination.
            — GRAHAM GREENE

I BUMPED along behind the two pilgrim lorries as they made their way into the fading light. Beside me were two females, an adolescent girl and her mother. They were relations of Aytha and he had asked me to give them a lift. They sat, two voluminous bundles completely covered in black cloth except for hennaed fingers and a pair of agitated eyes apiece. They complained of the heat.

'Take those veils off,' I demanded, 'no one can see you here except me, and I am a woman.'

Hardly assured but respecting my tone of authority, they removed the black headcloths. Both had round faces with light skins and the daughter was addicted to weeping. They fussed and twittered in the way of harem women and continued to complain about the heat.

'Why is the child so hot?' I asked at last. 'Is she feverish?'

They wagged their fingers backwards and forwards to indicate this was not the case, and the mother lifted the girl's black gown to reveal three other dresses below.

'For Heaven's sake,' I said, 'she is a walking wardrobe!'

Woman-like they refused to travel without extra clothes for after the pilgrimage they were staying with relations in Jeddah. But the girl would not remove anything and continued to complain, on the verge of tears, until a packet of sweet biscuits took her mind off her discomfort.

We were crossing the Musaiya Plateau that stands three thousand feet above sea level and as we topped a small rise we almost ran into three soldiers who were guarding a wrecked Saudi lorry. It had been returning from Attik, its mission unknown, when there was an ambush and the driver and his mate were killed. When they were found the lorry's cargo had disappeared.

I drove slowly, watching the struggles of the over-loaded lorries as they floundered in the sand. As soon as the vehicle began to falter the driver's assistants leapt down, grabbing the sand channels and pushing them in front of the wheels to give an extra grip. As the lorry moved, the men sprung forward to grab the freed channels again and throw them in front of the wheels once more. In this way the lorries were kept moving. It is a difficult procedure but anything is preferable to a dead stop, when the long business of digging out begins.

We had our first real breakdown at 9 p.m. when the smaller of the lorries suddenly stopped. The differential had broken.

'Have you a spare?' I asked Aytha. He shook his head. 'Then what will you do?'

'The large lorry goes back to al Abr for the spare part,' he said, unruffled.

Everything was taken from the large lorry and the other driver, Khomach, set off along the way we had come. The sand around us was now sprinkled with bundles, rugs, mats and the usual articles for making tea. Almost immediately pockets of fire sprung into life from small groups all over the sand. Others who had been standing in the lorries rolled up in rugs to sleep. The mother and daughter departed for more orthodox company, and as Hassan was nowhere to be found, I too rolled up in a rug and slept.

I woke to find Aytha and Hassan standing over me. The empty lorry had returned and now at 4.30 a.m. the repairs were finished. Already it had become clear that my Land-Rover was not going to give trouble in the sand and that instead of being a hindrance it could be useful. It was therefore agreed that our guide Mahammad Haradah would come in the Land-Rover with me, and we could go ahead looking for the best and safest terrain for the lorries. Hassan, delighted to get away from the rough swaying lorries insisted on coming too. The mother and daughter who had already installed themselves in the car were now ousted amid loud protestations and tears, which were silenced only by the appearance of Aytha.

Live Now – Die Later

Mahammad Haradah, the guide, belonged to the Damam tribe and came from Wadi Knabb in Yemen, an area within the fighting zone. He had come down with the two lorries on their previous journey and was now taking them back past the danger area again. He was a sparsely built young man with the tight drawn face of the desert Arab. Although he had never met a European woman he accepted me and the situation without any unease or surprise, and answered my questions about the area, giving various names, with patience and good humour.

We moved ahead through the black night and the three pools of light from the vehicles' headlamps became our conscious world. Should one disappear we were immediately on the alert. At the sand dunes near Um-ther-up when the lorries became stuck, we drove ahead and waited, watching their struggles which were dramatized in the two pools of light set in the deep black darkness. Soon after they were free we came to the well of Mushairiqa which is on the Darb al Amir and known to travellers for centuries. Philby speaks of the well and said that it had dried up when he passed this way thirty years ago and that repeated attempts had been made to find a new source, which no doubt was finally done, for a large concrete surround edges the well that today gives a good and abundant supply. Everyone topped up with water and dozens of agile figures climbed down the lorry's sides with their goat-skins and bottles; they flickered in and out of the car's lights chattering quietly.

In the darkness I tried to find the water sign Philby mentioned; twenty-eight dots and an armed man pointing to the well – enchanting! But no one could remember just where the old well had been.

We had covered only a few miles when we pulled up beside two huts. It was the first check-post. Aytha climbed down from his cabin with a large bunch of passports and permits and disappeared into one of the huts. He had not asked for my passport; perhaps he felt that until I had gone too far to be turned back, the less said about my presence the better! I sat in the Land-Rover enveloped in my kuffiyah and a soldier wandered over, flashing a torch at the front of the vehicle. The

72

Arabic lettering which had been added to the other numerals evidently reassured him and he wandered off again without even glancing into the car. Finally Aytha reappeared and as he passed the Land-Rover he gave me a quick glance before passing on. Was it a look of approval that I had remained inconspicuous? Had I been referred to? Perhaps Aytha, being known to the men at the post had been able to 'arrange things'? Whatever it was, the first hurdle had been taken.

We continued until the blackness paled and the edge of the earth showed around us, revealing a flat sandy plain. Behind us to the east was the distant range of Raiyan, a granite and basalt outcrop which we had passed during the night. The light strengthened and the sharp peaks of Jebel al Yass appeared on the horizon ahead. Slowly a line of hills began to form to our right, though around us the country was flat and bare. Except for the men at the check-post we had seen no one. Mahammad kept looking towards the sky as we drove along.

'What are you looking for?' I asked him.

'Planes,' he said and gave a graphic mime of planes releasing bombs.

'Already?' I was surprised.

We needed protection and the vehicles drove towards the peaks of Jebel al Yass, which were a series of peaked granite outcrops with large rounded boulders along the base. They made good camouflage for the vehicles and we spaced them well apart as a precaution. The pilgrims formed into small groups amongst the higher rocks.

From now on, as we were in the danger zone, we should be spending the daylight hours under cover, travelling only by night. The women, harem fashion, sought me out and settled near by. There were five women, three small girls and a baby. The boys stayed with their fathers. Hassan brought my camp bed, produced some hot water and then quickly disappeared. He had been unsuccessful in persuading anyone to cook for me and his look of horror when I suggested he do so resigned me to eating out of tins, and having the occasional meal with Aytha when we pooled our rations.

Left to ourselves on the east side of the hill we washed and generally tidied up, and the women wandered over to chat, drink tea and eat sweet biscuits. The pilgrimage was hard and difficult for them, with long hours in the swaying lorries in close proximity with so many strangers and with few opportunities of privacy as we were now enjoying. Finally I lay on my camp bed listening to the women's chatter which had become a quiet murmur; the baby cried ceaselessly and with a weary whine. The word *nasrani* was used often. I wished they would stop and allow the baby to sleep and finally I climbed round the rocks and took the small creature from its mother. She gave it to me apathetically for she was very tired. He stopped with surprise and I carried him back to my camp bed where he lay in the shade protected from flies by a chiffon scarf. Soon he ceased to cry and we all slept.

Later when the sun had lost its heat the mother came for the baby and I climbed amongst the boulders towards the summit. There were some rough and badly eroded inscriptions worked by travellers, resting as we were doing. The view from this height was magnificent, though empty and still. The immediate outcrops of black rock emerged from the white sand and beyond was the distant line of grey hills. The vast panorama of sky, streaked by white cloud was already softening to a faint rose. The still simplicity had the quality of a Japanese print. Silence framed the whole scene and nothing moved. Nothing? A tiny speck, advancing with the firm persistency not known to birds, moved across the sky. And now, cutting the silence came a tiny throb, faintly heard, then not – as though it struggled against the great weight of silence. On the sand below, men appeared running towards the women. They were seeking me also and turned in panic, questioning them. I cupped my mouth with my hands and gave a penetrating Australian 'cooee'. They looked up and motioned me to take cover then sped quickly back to the rocks. We sat, from our places of hiding, watching the tiny speck as it came nearer and nearer. The noise had now gained ascendancy and was dominating the whole scene. Once the rhythm changed and I caught my breath, as the others would, but the speck flew on and as we watched, disappeared out of sight towards the east.

Around five o'clock we moved cautiously on, skirting the other two hillocks which comprise Jebel al Yass, and turned south-west along a shallow wadi known as Hubail. The detour to the south is necessary because of the rising range of Jebel Hanger. Once again, three peaks appeared on the horizon ahead.

'What are they called?' I asked Mahammad.

'Ghas,' he murmured.

The two men sat beside me both slightly tensed and Mahammad looked frequently towards the sky. We were driving reasonably fast as the ground was quite firm. Between us and the hills to the right was a stretch of broken ground with boulders and stunted rak and acacia bushes. The hills beyond stood up high and solid and they stretched far ahead. It had been rumoured that somewhere in the mountains there was a Royalist Yemeni hide-out which had recently become the headquarters of the Imam el Bada himself. At one time the Republican army had advanced into these hills.

'Sallol was here,' said Mahammad.

'Sallol! The Republican leader?' I asked.

'Not now,' he said in a placating way. I hoped he was right. Suddenly he leant forward, '*Wallah!*' he said, looking towards the hills.

'What is it?'

Far to the right and already rising into the hills, was Aytha's lorry travelling at an incredibly fast speed.

'*Fi sah!*' shouted Mahammad indicating that I cut across the rough ground and give chase. Hassan's face had taken on a curious green tone. Explanations seemed out of place so I turned the Land-Rover towards the broken ground and the mountain, and we bounded across ridges and stones. Large sand mounds were missed by inches as Mahammad urged me on, but we were travelling behind the lorry's line of vision and finally were forced to strike out farther to the left to cut the vehicle off. The Land-Rover crashed dangerously over a fallen log and I groaned for my springs and axle. Finally we came within hearing distance and I sounded the horn. A pilgrim perched on the top seeing us, banged on the cabin roof and the lorry came to a standstill.

'What is all the fuss about?' I asked Hassan as Mahammad climbed out of the car and moved cautiously towards the lorry.

'All this ground leading to the hills is mined,' said Hassan flatly.

We started to retrace our steps, the Land-Rover leading. As we crossed the mined ground I tried desperately to follow my own tracks, though experience in similar fields has taught me that one can drive over a mine once and the second pressure sets it off. My companions sat very still, but they had, after all Allah to look after them!

As we neared Jebel Heth the light was beginning to fade and the sand formed into low rolling hills of semi-firm surface. Mahammad called a stop and climbed out of the vehicle, waiting for the two lorries to come abreast. Ahead lay a single track through the sand.

'From here,' said Mahammad, 'it is a minefield, it is danger-ous; we go *wahad wahad*,' and he left us to climb into Aytha's lorry which set off immediately.

The track had been made the hard way. All the mines had been exploded by passing vehicles. As we followed toe to tail, through the sand we almost touched shattered vehicles lying on distorted ground. We passed within inches of a huge round hole made by a bomb and had to edge round a lorry balanced precariously on its side. We moved slowly praying we would not stick. It was a curious drive in the fading light, a steady progress surrounded by destruction and war. Death was probably quite near, yet although there was tension – a strange waiting – there was no real fear. For *I* had my own acceptance of such eventualities and *they* had the faith of the inevitable rightness of Allah's will. We all had in our own way, the answer to living.

The daylight had gone completely before we were clear of the minefields and once through them Mahammad came back to the Land-Rover. His eyes gleamed in the light from the dashboard as he looked at me.

'*Tamam?*' he inquired and his desert-set face gave the nearest to a smile it could ever accomplish.

But the troubled difficult land gave us no respite and almost immediately we ran into sand dunes where the lorries stuck several times.

'No matter,' said Mahammad philosophically, 'it is now already Al Kharitah.'

The Army

Three hours later we came to a halt, pulling up in a row, to be immediately surrounded by people. Torches flashed, uniformed figures moved in front of the vehicles and soldiers peered at our faces. The air had lost its desert silence. There was stir and bustle as though people were everywhere and beyond was the sound of more activity. My heart gave a jump. Had we run into a battalion on the move? Were we – dreadful thought – surrounded by an advance Republican unit?

'Hello,' said a cheerful voice in excellent English, 'would you care for a cup of tea?'

7

Royalist Friends

Malo cum Platone errare, quam cum alus recte sentire —
— CICERO.

IT WAS the mountain headquarters of the Royalists and a
training ground for soldiers and mercenaries who would be
fighting in similar terrain.

Aytha came out of the darkness. 'Come,' he said. This was
evidently one of the places where I must make myself known.

We followed the young soldier Ali who spoke English. He
was a cheerful creature who had spent most of his life in Aden
and was delighted at the appearance of someone from those
parts. The ground was rough and we moved between large
boulders, over ground that was similar to the rocky outcrops
of Jebel al Yass. Finally we came to a shelter made of brush-
wood which led through to a small tent. Inside was an army
camp bed which Ali cleared of a heap of paraphernalia to allow
me to sit down. Two men sat on the ground behind a kerosene
lamp checking permits and Aytha joined them. Several old
men and a couple of soldiers came in and one by one they
shook hands, delighted at the company.

'I must go now,' said Ali, 'but I shall be back. They have
sent for the Imam's translator to help you. He speaks some
English.'

Almost immediately a slim pale-faced boy in his early teens
entered the tent. He was Abdul Aziz whose home was in Sana
which was now in Republican hands. His fine long features
contrasted with the round cheerful faces of the southern
Yemenis. He greeted me warmly. How fine to see me. Welcome! Welcome! He murmured the words with a gentle
maturity that was touching. He was leaving soon for Sana to
see his family, making his way behind the enemy lines. He was

too young to be involved in this cloak and dagger game that could mean death if he were caught.

Tea was brought, and biscuits in unopened packets which they pressed us to eat. Was there anything I needed? Orange squash? Cigarettes? They stood around, arms splayed, looking for further things to give. Their enthusiasm was infectious and if this was the losing side as some thought, no one would know it! But wasn't the chase, the excitement of war their common way of life, as it had been for the Hadhramis until the Peace made life safer – and duller? Perhaps war *is* necessary until other things are found to take its place.

The Yemen is the most fertile country in Arabia for its mountain range catches the monsoon rains and the mists that rise from the plains. A vast and ancient system of terracing which is highly efficient utilizes the mountainsides and makes the country extremely productive. Because of this there have been many invaders, the strong pushing the weaker down from the highlands, and most of these people forced into areas less fertile, moving with their herds in search of new pastures, became nomads. Today there are traces of the early Yemenis as far away as Najd, Syria and Iraq and because of this the country is often called the Cradle of the Arab.

Literally 'al Yemen' means 'the right hand' and some believe it is so named because the country lies to the right of Mecca when facing the east. Others believe that their ancestor Joktan, son of Eber, turned to the right when he and his followers were separated from the other Arabs. But a more likely explanation is that the words 'happiness' and 'prosperity' come from the same derivation as 'the right hand' and this beautiful country was known as Arabia Felix.

Waves of invaders came south across their country; the pre-Islamic kingdoms of the Minaeans, Sabaeans, Katabans and finally those boisterous and energetic Himyarites who established themselves here before moving and spreading south. Before these kingdoms there were the Hamites, though it is a name given collectively to tribes who wandered from southern Asia across Arabia and mingled with the Semetics here. From the first millennium B.C. they pushed south, but much of their history is still supposition; maybe they could be identified with the Land of Punt for the fine terracing was a characteristic of Punt.

It is not known for certain how early the Minaeans established themselves though about 700 B.C. they were pushed from their capital of Ma'in in Jauf by the invading Sabaeans. The Minaean kings had colonies to the north in Midian to protect their incense trade; and if Yemen was the land of Uz, and Job was a Minaean, then the tale of the Sabaeans having fallen upon his sons when they came as nomads through the country to the north, makes sense.

The Priest Kings of Saba pushed on south to establish their capital at Marib and they built the famous Marib dam whose ruins are still one of the wonders of the world, and evolved the irrigation system which spread over a vast area of Southern Arabia. Several smaller kingdoms existed at this time, each having a small portion of an area through which the Incense Route passed, but one by one they were absorbed when the Himyarites came to power. These were the last of the pre-Islamic dynasties and ancestors of the present Imam of Yemen who still brushes all documents with red ochre as a symbol of the Himyar princes. They appeared around 155 B.C., capturing the Sabaean capital of Marib and their princes assumed the title of Kings of Saba. By the fourth century A.D. they had absorbed the Katabans, Hadhramaut and most of the coastal lowlands. Many of the inscriptions and ruins found in Southern Arabia and the Yemen are attributed to these people who established a capital in Safar after the destruction of the Marib dam. Their last king Dhu Nowas, having taken the Jewish faith, persecuted the Christians and ordered a massacre at Najran, then a Christian stronghold, and thousands of Christians were killed. This, however, was his undoing for it led to the invasion in A.D. 525 of the Christian Copts from Abyssinia who defeated Dhu Nowas and killed him.

During the subsequent Abyssinian rule, Christianity spread all over the country, many churches were built and Najran became once more a Christian stronghold with its own bishop. The famous church at Sana built by Abraha an Abyssinian viceroy, rivalled Mecca as a place of pilgrimage. However, with his death Abyssinian rule weakened and the Persians, who had been infiltrating from the north, now installed themselves and appointed a Wahriz as Governor.

At first the Persians were tolerant towards the various religions, and Judaism, Christianity and the old astral worship all held their ground until in A.D. 628 when the Persian viceroy was converted to Islam and disturbances broke out. The Prophet's son-in-law Ali was sent south with a band of followers to try and convert all the people to Islam. He met with great success for much of the Islamic teachings suited the people and the way of life in the country. Finally this new Moslem world began to form into independent states and one of the first to do so was the Yemen where the new ruler Seif Allah claimed direct descent from Ali, and he in turn is the ancestor of the present Imams, who use the title Seif al Islam.

At this time an important event happened away in Iraq which was to affect the history and religion of the Yemen. It was the rise of the Zeidis and the dynasty of the Zeidi Imams, the sect which takes its name from one of Ali's grandsons.

The adherents of Ali can be confusing; the Shi'ah body of Mahammadans consist of many subdivisions, all recognizing Ali and his sons Hassan and Husein. The *main* body of Shi'ahs venerate a succession of Twelve Great Imams. It is the last of these Imams who disappeared and, it is believed, will reappear again as the Mahdi.

The Zeidis, however, differ as they recognize Zeid first and then venerate only the earlier of the Twelve Great Imams; after which they digress to Imams of their own. The first Zeidi, Zeid ibn 'Ali Zein al 'Abidin, who did not live in Yemen, was killed in A.D. 740 in Kufa in Iraq during an uprising against the Omeiyad Khalif. He became a martyr and from then on two separate bodies of Zeidi followers were formed, one group settled near the southern shores of the Caspian and the other was established in the Yemen and has survived to this day. The very first Zeidi Imam was Al Hadi ilal Hakk Yahya, grandson of Qasim ar Rassi who was descended in the sixth generation from Fatima and Ali and the house is known as the Rassite Dynasty. The inheritance does not always pass directly from father to son, for their heir must conform to many requirements amongst which is complete absence of any physical blemish, but without doubt they can claim direct descent from Mahammad the Prophet.

In the Middle Ages and also during the relatively recent Turkish occupation the Imams were merely spiritual rulers and it is only since the First World War that the Imam has become absolute ruler. It is small wonder that the country and its rulers have been loath to open their doors to the outside world.

'The Imam returns in less than four hours,' said Abdul Aziz, 'you must surely stay. He will be delighted to see you.'

If I stayed and let the convoy go on without me, I may not be able to continue along my route but have to retrace my steps; and I was supposed to be away from Yemeni territory! Also there was an especial affinity in being with the pilgrims who were making the journey as their ancestors had been doing over the centuries. We moved, as they had done, from one well to another; who can say at what distant time people passed along this route, carrying the incense which it was believed, gave a man's soul peace.

Aytha had not asked for my passport although one of the officers was murmuring that there was no *farangi* permit in the pile. Hardly a look passed between Aytha and myself but he took my lack of response as his cue. Should there by any possibility of us running into Republican troops it would be better that my passport had no Royalist stamp on it.

Ali returned to take us to meet 'The Generals' and we followed him out into the black night, climbing immediately up into the mountain. It became very steep and we scrambled from one boulder to another.

'You must stay and have dinner with us. We are going to kill a goat – in your honour,' said Ali as he pulled me up and over the crumbling mountain pass.

I doubted if nearly two hundred pilgrims could be asked to wait whilst the slow business of killing and cooking an animal went on!

It was a curious climb as we groped our way in the darkness. Finally we reached a narrow ledge and edged along towards an opening in the face of the rock. Two soldiers stepped aside to allow us to enter a large cave so brilliantly lighted with Tilley lamps that for a moment we stood stunned. The far inner wall of the cave had been hewn out, making two high and wide tiers that were covered with richly coloured carpets. On the higher ledge a massive man in the uniform of a general was looking at us.

'The General!' whispered Ali in my ear.

He was probably younger than his girth implied and gave the impression of having immense strength. His face was round and solid with a large moustache. He had a shock of unruly black hair. In his heavy black eyes was an expression of controlled patience and boredom – he seemed caged by the enforced inactivity. There were several other men sitting on the lower ledge or on the floor, their long gowns spread in a circle around them. An old general with a fine-lined face, a relative of the Imam, had an air of defeat as though he alone had knowledge of the futility of war. At the far corner, and slightly remote from the rest of the company, sat a man dressed in Russian-style tunic and trousers; he was writing with an air of profound detachment in a book. His yellow skin gleamed over thin, high cheekbones. Although he gave no indication of interest or disapproval at our visit, animosity radiated from that area of the cave.

I sat on the upper ledge beside the General and coffee was served. Having come from Aden I was accepted as an ally and our story never doubted. Was it my acceptance by the pilgrims or Aytha's good word that was responsible? The conversation, however, stayed on general terms.

In Najran they informed me I would be under the care of the Emir, Prince Khalid as Sudairi, who is one of Saudi Arabia's finest soldiers. It is natural that he should be in control of this troubled border town.

'They drop bombs on him,' said an old man with a ferocious gleam in his eyes, 'and he can no nothing. *We* are much luckier!'

'Bombs on him? But he's not at war!' I said.

' "They" drop them where they will,' he said.

Aytha was becoming restless for it was obvious we should be well away from this area before dawn.

Royalist Friends

'But in an hour the meal will be cooked!' wailed Ali as we rose to go.

'You could stay,' the General shifted his huge bulk to shake hands and the deep-set eyes seemed more relaxed.

'Thank you,' I said, but shook my head. 'Good luck,' I added, '– for your country.'

'And to you,' he said.

The old General regarded me intently and with a certain compassion; women had easier things to do than drive through war zones in the middle of the night.

We left the cave and moved cautiously down the mountain-side. At one particularly steep slide of rock I had to stand aside for a soldier who was climbing up carrying a large log.

'The firewood for your dinner,' said Ali disconsolately, 'pity! Never mind,' he added, his good humour triumphing, 'we have dinner some time – in Aden!'

I sat dozing in the Land-Rover. The night seemed endless; we had become involved in a miasma of long rolling dunes and the pilgrims had been unceremoniously turned out of the lorries and were making their own way over the sands. Ahead lay a long, shallow dip of sand through which the pilgrims moved, helped by the lights from the Land-Rover; they were passing us in straggling groups, and the lights revealed not only the tired figures but wrecked transport of all kinds; for we were passing through areas where battles had recently been fought. The lorries it seemed had lost heart also and Mahammad had gone back to help them out of the worst of the 'sticks'.

Hassan now had a bad cold and at regular intervals he opened the window and, using his hand, blew his nose out into the night. He was also extremely constipated and demanded large quantities of pills – all to no affect.

'Nothing,' he wailed continuously and miserably, 'nothing happens!'

His dreariness and lack of charm made me more impatient than the situation demanded and in this general deterioration I was lucky if occasionally my thermos was filled with hot water. I had long since given up any hope of eating anything but

The gateway to the sea, Bir Ali (Cana) with Husn el Ghourab in
the distance

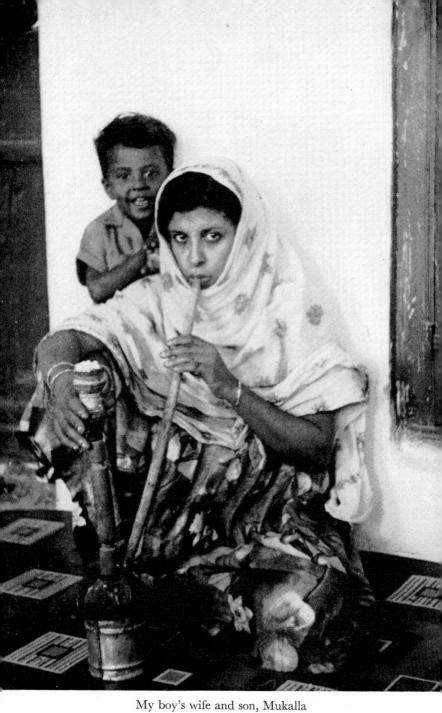

My boy's wife and son, Mukalla

A sheikh and his son in Wadi Jerdan, startled by my camera

Mubarak drawing water from a goatskin

A house in Seyuin

Seyuin

The young sheikh, Husn al Abr

The Emir of Tabuk, Hijaz

Mahammad the Damam guide and Aytha, with the pilgrim lorry, Yemen

A halt with the pilgrims in the Yemen

Huge ancient mortar, *Negrana Metropolis*, Wadi Najran

Near the source of Wadi Najran, Asir

The pilgrims leaving by ship from Jeddah

Slater, Riad, His Excellency German de Caso Ridaura and a local inhabitant at Khaibar

A group of Nabataean tombs on the western rocks, Madain Salih

Tomb used as a store by the bedu, Madain Salih

Slater changing a film in a Nabataean tomb, Madain Salih

An engine of the Hijaz Railway, in a shed at Madain Salih

The author, Faud and Brooks in a defile in Jebel Ethlib, Madain
Salih

Brooks and the author, Madain Salih

View from inside a Nabataean tomb and a carved capitol over 2,000 years old at Madain Salih

The author and some friends

The Emir of Hakl's secretary, the Emir and my guide Mahammad
leaving me at the Jordan border

cheese and biscuits and the servicing of the Land-Rover was completely ignored. I thought nostalgically of Mubarak who would have made the journey much easier and worth while.

Travelling with people needs discipline and concentration if one is to keep undiffused contact with the surroundings. Everything is more intensified when one is alone and a solitary month's journey is more vivid and remembered than many months in company. Just as with each journey a little more of the world is slotted into place, making a pattern and a smaller, more understandable whole, in which one is involved. Such is the web the constant traveller makes for himself; it is the creation and irony of the nomad, who becomes, more and more solitary with his increasing knowledge of the world.

Three men came into view moving slowly forward; two of them held the other older man by the arm and as they were level with the Land-Rover the old man sank to the ground.

I shook Hassan. 'Wake up, Hassan. What is the matter with the old man?'

'Huh?' He started and glanced out of the window.

It was a sad tale, told with many embellishments. The old man had fallen and knocked his head climbing out of the lorry. His friends had helped him so far but now his strength had given out. We put him on top of the jerrycans and boxes in the back but refused to take his companions for we were still very overloaded.

At this moment the two lorries came slowly up the slope and continued ahead into the sandy dip. We set off after them, our passenger groaning in the back. Later when the soft dunes were behind us, the lorries stopped for their passengers. I glanced back into the vehicle. The groaning had ceased and my passenger was spryly climbing out with no help from anyone. Hassan regarded me and the old man sourly. His mutterings, roughly translated, were: 'There is one born every minute!'

Opening my eyes I looked up into a fine tracery of acacia branches. There is something special in waking in an unknown place reached in darkness the previous night. Such times become engraved in the mind in a special kind of way. I have many such pictures; the Alhambra in Spain; the blue-grey of Pekin; Venice with the world of the canals coming to life; and the surprising brilliance of those other bluer waters of the canal at Timbuktu. Beside me now stood the Land-Rover, dusty but firm and all around were similar acacias, and rak and elb trees. They filled a wide flat wadi, whilst the mountain range of Weir rose on one side and the peaks of Shari on the other. We had stopped at 3.30 a.m. in Wadi Knabb which has its beginning in the Yemen hills, and finally expends itself in the sands of the Rub el Khali in the east.

We were on much the same route as Philby took in 1932 when he made his remarkable journey from Najran to Hadhramaut. Of the route he remarked: '. . . and on this line it can scarcely be doubted that we have one of the several routes followed by the ancient spice trade of Arabia Felix'.

It was near here also that the French explorer Halévy was abandoned by his guides in 1869 when on his way back from the ancient city of Marib. His search for the route taken by the Roman, Aelius Gallus and his army in the first century B.C. had been fruitless, but perhaps he was also looking for the renowned treasures of Arabia Felix as the Roman had been. Tales of riches and treasure tend to become exaggerated, and such tales led to the disastrous expedition when the Emperor Augustus sent Aelius Gallus from Egypt to Saba in 24 B.C. It was his intention to make the country a dependency of Egypt and his force of 10,000 men included soldiers sent by Herod and also the Nabataean king. The company landed in Arabia at Leuke Kome, two hundred miles north of present-day Jeddah, and marched south-east for nine hundred miles along the eastern slopes of the Yemen highlands; though to have landed farther south along the coast would have saved the tough and waterless trek. Except for this hardship they met with their first serious opposition in Wadi Najran where they attacked the oasis and gained a victory. Later, advancing farther south, they took Athula and Nasca but seem to have gone east of Marib and were finally forced to turn back from lack of water.

This unhappy venture changed the outside world's opinion of the peninsula and the tales of untold wealth and of the fertility of the territory in Arabia Felix were naturally modified,

Lunch in Wadi Knabb

for Gallus had not seen the green, lush lands of Shabwa and Hadhramaut. The journey south had taken six months and the return only sixty days; and so it could be argued that the expedition was sabotaged from the start. Gallus's guide was Syllaeus, the Vizier of the Nabataean king of Petra; and had the undertaking succeeded and the source of Arabia's wealth been found, Petra would have suffered greatly from loss of trade. Until then all caravans going to Egypt and Syria passed through the Nabataean capital.

We were 4,000 feet above sea level and the air was crisp and clear. The pilgrims had already dispersed in groups along the wadi and amongst the rocks, and I set about having a wash. We now had a working arrangement whereby when I put my red plastic jerrycan on the Land-Rover's bonnet, it was an indication that I was about to have a wash and the pilgrims kept away. Later I brought out my first-aid kit in readiness for patients. There was always someone with a blister, a cut finger, a headache or constipation. An aspirin or two would cure a headache but constipation was my most stubborn enemy and I was congratulated delightedly when my remedies worked. Others who had little wrong with them came for treatment and were pleased to go off with a couple of pills wrapped in a spotless Kleenex tissue. The whole convoy showed signs of my efforts for there was a goodly rash of Elastoplast stuck on the dark skins which they managed to keep amazingly clean.

At noon we gathered under a large acacia tree for a meal of rice coloured with saffron, tuna fish and onions. Now for the first time since leaving Husn al Abr we saw bedouin, and three men of the Yam tribe joined us for lunch. They were lean and strong looking with a ruggedness not found in the Hadhramis; they wore futah and shirts and their hair was shorter than my companions. Each carried a large and extremely old rifle. As well as the Yam there was Aytha, Khomach the driver of the other lorry, Hassan, Mahammad, two elderly pilgrims, Aytha's father and myself.

This was Yemeni territory, the country of the Dahm tribes and although the Yam owe allegiance to Saudi Arabia and their territory extends from the north around the wells of

Najran and far out into the desert, they bring their flocks wherever the grazing is good. The gossip had a dramatic tone with stories of bombing, sniping and infiltration from both sides. Yesterday planes had come over from the west and dropped bombs in the wadi killing four bedouin. The men were incensed and disgruntled at such methods of warfare which was so impersonal. To them, the death of a person should be paid for in kind – or at least with money. Wars, it seemed, had deteriorated. It was, one suspected, the fault of the *nasrani*. They looked at me balefully.

Where, they asked, had I come from? Aden! *Wallah!*

'It is not good,' said our youngest visitor, 'for a woman to travel alone.'

One of the old pilgrims looked at me disparagingly. 'It is nothing,' he said with scorn, 'she is old.'

There was a murmur of disbelief from the others and Mahammad shook his head, smiling with a touch of embarrassment at such lack of manners. But the old man was adamant; he was not to be fooled.

'Of course she is,' he said, spurred on by their disbelief, 'she must be thirty years!'

'*Shukran!*' I smiled at him. He looked startled by my reaction. Not only passé, but senile, his manner implied!

So much of life can be spoilt by the wrong attitude to those advancing years; to meet them half-way, seeing the advantages, using the experience, to say nothing of the pleasure of being able to relax a little, can make it an especial kind of adventure.

The district of Jauf lay a little to the west of our present position; here the ruins of Ma'in with its temples and great circular tombs lie. They have been seen by few people although Halévy called them 'some of the most spectacular in Arabia'.

'Could I go to Jauf while we are waiting here?' I asked.

'*Musch mumpkin!*' they said with one accord.

'But why not?' I asked. 'I would never be seen by planes in this wooded wadi.'

'The Republicans are there, even the pilgrims keep away,' they assured me.

Suddenly the men raised their heads and listened. From

The Bomber

behind the hills to the west came the sound of a plane's engine. We stood up, as all along the wadi groups of pilgrims who had been sheltering under the trees rose to their feet and began to move silently towards the rocks. The clear still day had become ominous. Aytha walked beside me with his usual slow movements, his inscrutable face lost in thought. We were the last to arrive at the base of the hill and moved between the high boulders. The wadi was empty now, and the spreading branches of the large acacias formed a great canopy over the sand. My Land-Rover stood under one of them and I hoped the reflection from the glass wasn't too conspicuous. The beautiful day seemed ill-equipped for sudden destruction and death. How odd it would be to become a casualty in such a place. Suddenly, with a heightening of sound the plane came into view immediately above us. It was a bomber flying reasonably high, but once over the centre of the wadi it altered course and started to move along it. Aytha glanced at me as we stood leaning against a large boulder and a faint flicker of interest, of query, showed on his face, as though he found my self-contained attitude surprising.

The plane circled lower now and the drone of the engine was the only sound. The Land-Rover looked terribly conspicuous. '*Allah karim*,' I murmured and Aytha smiled. The plane was almost parallel with us now, but suddenly with an upward spurt it climbed again and flew away, disappearing over the ridge of the hills towards the east.

'What now?' I asked Aytha, but before he could answer there was a sudden report of ack-ack guns from the neighbouring wadi; a second spurt, and almost immediately came the deadening crunch of bombs – and then there was silence.

8

Sheba Came This Way

The still, sad music of humanity.
— WORDSWORTH

MAHAMMAD CAME to the end of the wadi; he had brought us through the difficult part of his tribe's territory and was now returning to his people. We stopped the vehicles where the wadi ran towards high folds of sand and he and Aytha climbed out of the lorry. They spoke about the difficult dunes ahead and then they said 'good-bye' Dahm fashion, placing their palms together without clasping hands and, leaning forward, touched noses six times. It was a solemn and unhurried ritual, a firm declaration of comradeship and of a job well done.

Mahammad had been surprised and pleased with the hundred-shilling contribution I gave him as our guide, and now he came over.

'Come back,' he said, 'bring the "gazelle" and we will go to Dawasir.'

'Ah, *insha allah* – it is possible.'

'With the "gazelle", all is possible,' and he was gone.

We drove off into the sunset and had not gone far when shots rang out from the bushes near by. The trigger-happy bedouin were taking pot-shots at us! I swung the Land-Rover to one side and barely missed running over an unexploded shell which was sticking up in the sand.

'*Allah karim!*' I said to the sleeping figure of Hassan beside me.

We ran for a while along Wadi Itema and the shaggy hills of Dhara rose to the west. The massif of Hadhra lay between us and the desert. The high Yemeni mountains taper off towards the east and the rocky outcrops stretch out into billowing sands so that it resembles a long coastline.

'Why Didn't You Stop?'

It was dark when we reached our next check-post, an isolated and crude shack set on the side of a sand sea. I pulled up, convoy fashion, between the two lorries and followed my usual procedure of staying put, swathed in my kuffiyah. Our stops at the check-posts near the fighting area were sometimes quite long for the Yemeni authorities scrutinize the pilgrims' permits thoroughly. A republican *could* be smuggling himself in under the guise of a pilgrim! After the good reception at army headquarters I was not expecting trouble, but after a short time Aytha came towards me and with a gesture indicated that I go on ahead. I was surprised for the sand was very soft, the place isolated and, what was more, I had no idea which direction to take in the dark. Knowing Aytha must have a reason I put the Land-Rover into gear and set off past his lorry.

We had not gone more than ten yards in the soft sand when I saw in my driver's mirror, someone flashing a torch behind us.

'Hassan! What does it mean? The flashing torch?'

'It means to stop.'

So that was it! Aytha wanted me out of the way and evidently the post had no vehicle to give chase.

'I can't stop,' I said, 'in this soft sand; I would never start again.'

'*Marlish!*' he had the Arab's democratic approach to officialdom.

Later when we all stopped to make tea Khomach came up to me. 'Why didn't you stop?' he demanded. 'Didn't you see the torch flashing?'

'Yes.'

'Flashing torches always mean "stop". The police had no vehicle to follow you and we couldn't catch you.'

'Why did they want me?'

'It is prohibited for a small vehicle to go further. It cannot get through the sands of Taiyib el Ism. They wanted to send you back.'

'Send me back! The Land-Rover hasn't stuck yet!'

'That is what Aytha said.'

I understood their attitude a little better when we arrived at the dunes of Taiyib el Ism, for they were huge and quite chaotic, a jumble of dunes that mazed in every direction. But it was the lorries as usual that had difficulty and after many hours we came to an impasse where the ground rose ahead in a great wall of sand. The name 'Taiyib el Ism' is given to many places whose terrain beggars description for it means 'that's a good word for it'.

Khomach came over as I drew up. Since Mahammad had left us, Khomach had taken the position of second-in-command to Aytha. 'Stay here,' he said, 'and after I have taken the lorries over, I shall come back for you.'

Three hours later he returned. 'I run ahead,' he said, 'you follow me.'

'But, Khomach, I shall have to rush the dune, you cannot go that fast!'

'Follow!' he demanded; his thin, bony face gleamed like bronze in the car's lights and he smiled encouragement.

It would be a disaster should I stick, for the smaller vehicle would dig very deep into the soft dune. Khomach rushed the rise ahead of us; like some mystical *jinn* he sped over the sand, his long shirt and kuffiyah flying. I gathered speed to combat the rise and his feet seemed to barely touch the ground. We moved steadily on towards the top when suddenly I lost him out of the line of light. For a moment I panicked, not knowing which way to turn. Below me loomed a deep drop of sand, perhaps a precipice, for I could not see its depth, but at this moment Khomach's flying figure swung into vision again to the left and I edged the vehicle towards him. We gained speed as the dune began to fall away towards firm ground again, below us.

He stood, panting, beside me. 'Thank you, Khomach.' He merely grinned, and set off across the sand to his own lorry.

I drove in a haze. We had not stopped to rest or to eat, and my back ached. Hassan was asleep beside me and there was nothing but the rattling vehicle – and the light beams ahead. The stars were hard and near, and strangely persistent as we drove on, ahead of the others, over the even surface of Wadi Afrain. It went on and on, flat as a billiard table. The stars, strange moving stars, were coming nearer and nearer . . . they approached and began to change, no longer stars but dancing figures, sideways half figures, turned, it would seem, side on; half a body with one eye, one leg, one arm. They danced towards me, enveloping me; and all around was a great shimmering maze of gold . . .

I woke with a start and in a panic. I had stopped! But with no recollection of having done so. The other vehicles? Had they driven past me and were now miles ahead of us? My eyes were becoming accustomed to the gloom as an edge of light showed to the east. Around me on the sand were many long dark logs, the familiar wrapped-up bundles of our pilgrims. Beyond stood the two lorries. I must have brought the Land-Rover to a halt just as I was falling asleep and Aytha, finding me, had called a halt. The bare landscape was becoming grey but the half figures had gone. Why had I dreamed of the one-eyed *jinnun* who inhabit the lost city of Wabar? It was lost when the people of 'Ad and Thamud were destroyed, and legend has it that this is where the gold of Arabia came from and that the *jinnun*, one-eyed, one-legged and one-armed, guard it to this day. Was this the city Aelius Gallus was looking for, two thousand years ago? You will be told that it lies somewhere between Shabwa and Dhufar country, a vast area in which to look. When Philby crossed the Rub el Khali his guides took him to a place near Al Rima on the southern edge of the great desert which they believed was Wabar. He found several large meteorites that were twisted into fantastic shapes resembling odd structures but it was no man-made city. Philby also spoke of ruins and a permanent well called Uwaifira, a two-day camel-ride east of the area we were now passing through, and although he could not visit it, he believed this was a possible place of identification for Wabar. Some believe great tiredness and pain makes one susceptible to outside influences, that pain breaks through the wall of conscious living – perhaps we were nearer Wabar than we knew!

We were nearing Saudi Arabian territory, the worst dangers were over and we could travel by day. There was an easing of tension and a festive air about the pilgrims. The lorries moved with reckless abandon along the giant ridges or claws that spread out into the desert from Wadi Hiswa. Often we were forced to turn back along the ridge when they ran into soft sand, but over the final ridge a great plain confronted us. To the west lay the old watering place of Maiain with the mountains of Yemen beyond. On the plain one of the lorries had a puncture and we stopped for an hour whilst the wheel was being changed. Immediately the community fell into shape as groups set about making tea. My regulars came for aspirin, vitamin tablets and cascara pills, or for the final change of Elastoplast. An old man brought his wife, she was a tall gaunt woman with a still, withdrawn air. Her eyes were bloodshot and streaming from the glare and she fought the disability with an odd sense of outrage. Knowing that tracoma can spread with the indiscriminate use of ointments, I offered her a spare set of sun glasses, only to find later that her eyes were still streaming – and her husband was wearing the glasses!

Hassan's cold was worse and he demanded more aspirin, as well as the regular doses of pills for constipation.

'It is useless, Hassan,' I said, 'one cancels the other out. Either take aspirin for your cold, or pills for your tummy. Which is worse?'

He threw up his hands and lurched off; somehow it was all my fault!

As I moved between the groups several of them asked me to share their tea or a meal, delighted when I accepted. How long will the traditional hospitality of the Arab last in the modern world? Generosity is a prime virtue to them and a man who dies poor because of his generosity is honoured above all others. One will find an old man, now destitute, who had been very rich and he is treated with great deference, almost reverence, and his acts of generosity recounted as tales of great valour. There was the old sheikh whose flocks were dead and he had nothing left but his horse. A friend who had repeatedly tried to buy the horse called once more and was invited by the sheikh to stay for a meal. Later, knowing his host was almost destitute the friend offered an even larger amount for the horse; but the old sheikh shook his head replying, 'You are indeed generous; but, my friend, we have just eaten my horse.'

One of the lads had been sitting for a long time completely absorbed in a book. 'Is it a good book?' I asked.

The Saudi Border Guard

He looked up vaguely, reluctant to bring his mind away from the absorbing story.

'Is it good?' I repeated.

'Oh, *very* good!' he now said with enthusiasm. He closed it to show me the cover, which although in Arabic, seemed familiar. It was a copy of *The Three Musketeers*!

It was not necessary for the vehicles to stay together from here to the wells of Khudra in Wadi Najran for the way was flat and uncomplicated.

'Come,' said Khomach to me, 'let us go on ahead'. He had been engaged for the journey to Najran and then he had another job that would take him north-east to Riyadh. The sooner he reached Najran the better.

The plain was studded with low bushes and Khomach was keeping far to the left moving at great speed, when suddenly from the right a small white vehicle appeared which was moving quickly towards us.

'Saudis!' said Hassan beside me.

'Saudis?'

'Saudi border guards.' He proffered the information with a mixture of exasperation and respect.

The vehicle drove ahead of Khomach's lorry and stopped dead in its path. We both pulled up with a jerk as a good-looking Saudi Arabian officer, fury written all over his face, climbed out of the vehicle and walked back towards Khomach.

'Don't you know there is a check-post over there?' pointing towards the way he had come, 'I have come right out of my way to catch you!' he added angrily.

Khomach made a placating gesture which the furious officer waved aside.

'Don't you realize I am wasting petrol, coming all this way after you?'

This shook me. Previously the Saudis would have considered it out of place and vulgar to mention such economies as they were luxuriating in their country's new-found wealth. I went over and stood beside Khomach hoping the officer's attack might be averted.

'My name is Barbara Toy,' I said, rather ineffectually.

Sheba Came This Way

He looked down at me. 'You are late,' he said. 'We have been expecting you for two weeks.'

Efficient as well as frugal!

'Khomach was bringing me along; but what with the bombs . . .' I trailed off.

The handsome face had lost its angry flush though the eyes regarded me distantly; then a familiar look of masculine patience crept into them; women *always* caused eruption, it was a cross to be borne. With a grand gesture, having made his point, he waved us on.

I was suddenly overwhelmingly glad to be here with the Saudis again; for they are not a niggardly race and have the confidence that stems from breeding. But I wondered what awaited me at the border town of Najran for Aden had warned that I should probably be met and escorted all the way through the country. Also I had not dared to inquire if the old law that forbids women to drive vehicles was still in force in the country.

Already the desert had lost its singularity, though we had seen no one but the Saudi officer, and we passed Khartam Sara, a long ridge of dark granite, and came to Ukt where a camp of the International Red Cross was set up beneath a huge outcrop of heavily eroded rock. Though their main purpose was to help the casualties of the Yemen civil war, they were giving assistance to the pilgrims as they passed through. The old wells of Khudra lie in the wadi east of Najran and as far back as earliest recorded history all routes from the south passed this way. The Queen of Sheba brought her camels and elephants to be watered here when she came through on her way to visit King Solomon; perhaps her caravan climbed these shallow sandy hills we were now approaching, to give their queen her first glimpse of the great wadi beyond. As we reached the top the wadi stretched below us; it was already widening towards the desert and below on the sloping, sandy banks many groups of pilgrims sheltered under the picturesque umbrella acacia trees. Beyond to the east was a cluster of peaked granite boulders with two buildings and some shacks near by.

We sheltered under one of the trees until late afternoon and a continuous stream of pilgrims passed us on their way to the wells. Some of the pilgrims stopped having heard I was a *tabib*. A group of women edged near and one of them was holding her head and groaning; they were aghast when I beckoned her over before attending to the men present; but woman-like they quickly adjusted to the new status and became even more demanding and garrulous than the men.

It was decided to send me on ahead to Najran for it would take a day to check all the pilgrims through the customs. I drove with Hassan towards the buildings. Beside the Emir's enclosure was the house of the customs official. He was an old man in a long white dishdasher and with a coloured kuffiyah, rather awry on his head. I was a novelty, a change from the pilgrims and he followed me out to the Land-Rover and insisted on having the *entire* contents of my expedition out on the sand. Everything was opened and he went through box after box, garment after garment until my small world from nightdresses to motor spares, was displayed before us; to the great interest and delight of every man and boy within sight. Was it just inquisitiveness or did he think I would be foolish enough to bring spirits into the country? This is a stringent law which if broken can be punishable by death. I was beginning to lose patience when the unpleasant exhibition was brought to a close by the appearance of the Emir. He was a kindly old man with no interest in any of my things and after inviting me to visit the harem later, wandered off taking the old official with him; it took over an hour to make some sort of order out of the chaos created.

Inside the enclosure of the Emir's establishment was an inner wall jutting out into the centre of the courtyard, and a badly erected curtain on a rod continued across the remaining space cutting off the harem from the rest of the area. We went first into the *maglis* which was a long narrow room backing the outer wall with an incongruous row of tubular chairs set along the wall. We were served coffee from the traditional slender-necked brass pot whose deeply curved spout and pointed lid come straight out of the *Arabian Nights*. The tiny handleless cups are half filled and custom demands that after the third cup you shake it from side to side as you hand it back, to denote you have had enough; should you omit to do this, coffee will continue to be served to you *ad infinitum*! People wandered in, some to speak to the Emir, others to take coffee and to look at the stranger. The Emir's secretary, a business-like young man, had many queries about me and the pilgrims. The Emir was reluctantly caught up in the new accelerated pace; and formally the process of sending me on to the Emir of Najran, with a letter of introduction, would have taken two or three days, but now the secretary chivvied him into writing the letter before I had finished my three cups of coffee.

Finally the Emir rose, the task completed. 'Come,' he said to me, 'we go to the harem'; and he led me behind the curtain.

There were four women, three small boys and a sick baby. They were all pale skinned and sallow. Each of the boys had a cold and the baby was flushed with fever. The women wore plain black gowns that trailed on the dusty courtyard and black scarves covered their heads. They were devoid of any animation except for a highly strung tension often found amongst the women of the harem. They asked me for pills for the usual complaints and were surprised that I was not a doctor and so could do nothing for the baby. If I was not a doctor, why was I taking such an uncomfortable journey? Was I making the pilgrimage? They put the baby in my arms. She was as light as a rag doll and burning hot through her scant clothes. I tried to persuade them to take her into Najran or to the Red Cross unit at Ukd, but the suggestion was met with no response. Either previous visits had proved useless or it was mere laziness. Their portion of the courtyard was bare except for a crudely made stone stand for cooking and their rooms were a clutter of tin boxes, rugs and cushions. Their apathy and boredom was depressing but understandable for their surroundings, from which they seldom escape, were dreary.

When we left, the Emir took me to the granite boulders where in a pocket of sand in the centre some of his contemporaries were grouped round a fire. The Emir relaxed as we sat sipping tea; the transition to the fast pace of today is difficult for such people and here they have few of the resulting advantages. The men spoke about the desert and of the journey to the south; and invariably St. John Philby's name was mentioned. They were not surprised that I should know him, for weren't we both British? The Emir had accompanied him on one of his journeys.

'Philby told me about your wadi and spoke about the ruins of Negrana Metropolis,' I said.

'He would search always for old stones,' said the Emir.

I met St. John Philby in Riyadh on my previous visit to Saudi Arabia. He had regarded me with his intent uncompromising stare: 'You are young and will travel to many places. Try to reach Najran, it was one of the greatest of the Sheba cities, both in size and importance; and it is also one of the loveliest oases in the world.' He spoke of the wadi breaking through the mountains towards the desert, of the black hills surrounding it, setting off the vivid green of the alfalfa and millet.

When Philby visited Najran in 1936, Joseph Halévy was the only other European to have seen it for many centuries, though its name was well-known through Arab scholars and historians. Philby's route had been much the same as my own except that he did it in reverse, for he came down from the Mediterranean and continued south to Hadhramaut. His was the first motor vehicle to accomplish the journey, but the expedition was sponsored by the king and consisted of a retinue of soldiers and guides.

Prince Khalid as Sudairi, the Emir of Najran, elected to live under canvas out in the centre of the wadi rather than in the town. Sudairi is a famous name in Saudi Arabia and its sons have produced many fine administrators and governors. The family originally came from Dawasir and had their seat in Sudair in Najd for generations. Many of them have married into the royal family and the present king's father, Ibn Saud, had a Sudairi mother. Prince Khalid's exploits as a soldier and administrator form part of Saudi history, and his appointment as Emir in this troubled border town was an obvious one.

We were making our way down the wadi in search of the Prince's camp and beside me sat an askari with a letter of introduction to him. The camp was difficult to find and we became involved in a labyrinth of tracks that ran through heavily wooded ground. Finally we pulled up in front of an elaborate cluster of large tents well camouflaged amongst the trees. We waited some time whilst the askari went in search of information.

He returned at last. 'Come,' he said, 'the Emir is away, and we must go to the city gates. His secretary will meet us.'

In the darkness we made our way towards the city whose Christian massacre is one of the undisputed pieces of Arabia's history; it is vouched for by Arab and occidental writers as well as by the Koran. The Jesuit king who was known as 'The Lord of the Curls' had large pits dug in which a huge fire was started and the victims were murdered and thrown into the fire. They included priests, monks, women and children, 10,000 in all. Najran's bishop, Paul Arethas, the ruler of the town, was imprisoned and later beheaded and his wife Ruma was compelled to taste the blood of her two slain daughters before being murdered herself. Today when bones are dug up around the ruins of Ukhdud (Negrana Metropolis) they are believed to be those of the Christian martyrs.

An hour later the last Christian drew up in front of the high and sombre arch of the eastern gate of Najran.

9

The Waking Giant

A man clothed in a *clacca* to his eyes, whose brows touch
Heaven.   – C. M. DOUGHTY

THE EMIR'S secretary Ali was handsome and elegant in a
long white gown, tailored jacket and snow-white kuffiyah. He
stood framed by the archway of the old gate, ready to escort me.
His form of transport was a Toyota, a small Japanese four-
wheel-drive vehicle, more like a Jeep than a Land-Rover. The
ownership of one of these uncomfortable little vehicles is a
status symbol in these parts.

'You will be hungry,' he said sensibly, 'follow me,' and
returning to the Toyota was off at breakneck speed.

It was a terrifying journey as we tried to keep the vehicle
in sight. The track was badly corrugated and high speed was
the only safeguard against skidding. A few vehicles swept past,
missing us by inches as we took the sharp corners; and after
five miles, which seemed like twenty, we came to an open
space that ran towards the market square. The Toyota pulled
up short of the square beside a low windowless building with
one door. Ali climbed out of his vehicle and came across to us.

'This is the restaurant,' he said, 'the best in town,' and led
me through the door.

The long low room was bare of ornaments. Tables and chairs
were set along the walls and at the far end were a large refriger-
ator and a counter. Several clients, all men, sat at the tables;
some wore European-style trousers and shirts, but others had
retained the traditional long white gown and kuffiyah. There
was a pleasant air of workmanlike efficiency and good service,
and to one who had been living on coffee and biscuits for many
days, the odours coming from the kitchen were very welcome.

The Waking Giant

'The food is good,' said Ali, 'the place is run by a Palestinian.' He glanced at me quizzically and at the men at the tables; generations of custom prevailed. 'Come,' he said, and led me through the room to an inner court.

Ali had gazelle-like eyes, common to many Saudis, who despite their masculinity have gentle manners. They are attractive men and pure blood gives them an easy superiority, which made the Saudi of the desert in his flowing gown and swathed features, inscrutable, romantic and inaccessible. Now the modern, sophisticated ones have lost their remoteness and can communicate more easily, which makes them devastating to the opposite sex.

We sat at the table in the little court which was filled with crates of empty bottles, boxes and tins. A couple of dusty plants were struggling to grow in the dry sand.

The proprietor was a large fair-skinned man with resigned, sad eyes. He had been forced to leave his home after the Palestine war and had come south to Najran with his brother who now ran the bakery next door. Both of them had the education and intelligence to do more skilled work, but they were working hard and making money.

We were given large plates piled high with grilled kidneys, fried eggs and chips. Non-alcoholic beer, in a bottle which was a faithful replica of the more potent kind, was put before us. It had a horrible taste but the bottle looked good on the table.

Much later we drove to the Prince's guest house, where an old man, holding a lantern, helped me through the little inset door and led the way across a huge courtyard, sombre in the shadows except for the dim pool of light from the moving lantern. At the far side was a room with a large iron bedstead. I climbed on to it – and slept for eleven hours.

The caretaker had been sitting outside my room for some hours. He was dressed in a long white dishdasher with a revolver in a heavy holster strapped round his hips. He was an old soldier and his appearance was made fierce by a deep gash across his face which looked as though it was hewn out of granite. He was dignified and had great authority, and was waiting to accompany me to the Diwaniyya. First, however, he gave me some strong sweet tea, flat bread and honey.

The guest house had thick high walls which enclosed the large inner court. Around the walls were several rooms opening to the court. There was a bench for washing and near by a room with a lavatory and open draining to the wadi below. Steps ran up to a platform or gallery-roof which had sections of mud walls, for it was used for sleeping in the summer months. The building is on the outskirts of the town and the space in front of the house could only be called a road because two walls, thirty feet apart, run parallel with each other. Palms rose from behind the walls and beyond were the blue-grey hills. The house next door was occupied by the Royalist Yemenis and their heavy outer door was kept securely bolted. There was a slight 'cloak and dagger' atmosphere about the few people who entered or left the house, which was in complete contrast to the easy atmosphere of those down in the fighting zone.

There is no clutter about present-day Najran, it spreads over a large area which makes its growth and the resulting building so much easier. It splays out into the wadi to a fringe of beautiful gardens which are set in fine old mud walls. The main square is edged with buildings, the same colour as the ground, which are shops and offices and in the centre is a lively market where everything can be bought from saddles to spices and clothes. Many of the stalls exchange money as well.

The old main street runs along the north side of the square and has the town's largest and finest buildings. It continues east where new mechanics' workshops, a petrol station and other modern buildings are springing up. One space has been left clear for the pilgrims and their lorries, and near by is a large bare house, also for the pilgrims, with empty rooms and washing facilities from a well in the court of the house. Beyond is a new concrete hospital, well equipped but waiting its staff and doctors.

We drove to the Diwaniyya which lay off the main street and climbed the steps past tall guards standing around with easy informality. How should I be treated? To have obtained a visa at all was just one of those lucky breaks, but to arrive in my own vehicle at such an outpost was unorthodox to say the least. However, there was probably no precedent and this could work in my favour, as no woman, I was sure, had driven a vehicle into Najran from the south.

The mudir, a young man from the north, greeted me pleasantly. He sat behind a modern metal desk in a long room lined with chromium chairs, which looked incongruous when the dignified gentlemen in spotless thorb and white kuffiyahs sat on them. As each man came in he walked directly to the mudir to greet him before passing round the room to shake hands with the rest of the company, murmuring greetings and repeating the same phrases over and over again when coming to a special friend. Some included me in the ceremony but others quickly put their sleeves over their hands before offering it to me, whilst others again declined to touch me at all.

Coffee, tasting pungently of ginger, was served from a brass coffee pot whose spout had a filter of palm fibre. After the coffee the usual three cups of tea were served.

The Chief of Police, a small dark man who spoke perfect French, arrived and for the first time since leaving Seyuin my passport was inspected.

'You must see the Emir soon,' said the mudir, 'and in the meantime you are our guest. Anything you should want . . .?'

I thanked them and said I would like to see the old city of Ukhdud.

'*Wallah!*' said the Chief of Police thumping the table, 'then you are an excavator!'

'No,' I said, 'I am not a professional – excavator. Just an amateur.' But they would have none of that, and from then on I was Sir Mortimer Wheeler, Kathleen Kenyon and Professor Mallowan, all rolled into one!

The old men looked on and the fanatical Wahhabi glint showed in many of the proud eyes. But when we rose to go and I passed down the long line, although there were disapproving faces, they were polite. A few years ago a Christian would need protection here and even today the town is fiercely Wahhabi.

One shy Arab from Palestine sought me out. 'I have a secret,' he said, glancing round carefully. 'You see, I too, am a Christian.'

The Four Provinces

'Oh,' I said, 'and does it matter?'

'Oh yes, it is better not to say, when you are an Arab. But it is so lonely to be the only one,' he smiled shyly. 'Oh, how I wish you could stay,' he added ingenuously.

Saudi Arabia's four provinces, Hijaz, Asir, Najd and Hasa cover territory that stretches across the peninsula from the Red Sea to the Persian Gulf. Jordan and Iraq border the north and to the east is Kuwait, Qatar, the Trucial Coast and the Persian Gulf. The coastline of the Red Sea and a small part of the Yemen form the western border, whilst to the south the Rub el Khali forms a natural boundary.

The Hijaz runs along the Red Sea for seven hundred miles and has a coastal plain that varies in width from twenty to forty miles. It is backed by the mountain range that continues south into Asir where it becomes extremely rugged and often almost impregnable. Najd, with Riyadh as the national capital, is known as the 'Heart of Arabia' and is the largest province. A high plateau runs down the centre from the Tuwaiq Mountains to the province of Hasa. Najd was the original home of the Sauds and the centre of the austere and fanatical Wahhabi sect which helped to put Ibn Saud in power. Although Hasa is the smallest province it is the wealthiest, for like its neighbour Kuwait, it has oil. It was, however, rich in comparison with the rest of the country before the discovery of oil, for the fertile and abundant Hofuf oasis lies within its borders.

The story of Ibn Saud, the present king's father and his rise to power is well known when, with the Wahhabi's help, he brought most of Arabia under his control. He was a man of the desert and his bedu statesmanship made it possible for him to consolidate his victories, whilst his natural good sense helped him to cope with the preliminary responsibilities that the discovery of oil brought. Towards the end of his life however he found difficulty in adjusting to the wild commercialism and seeming ungodliness of the twentieth century. His son, King Faisal, has many of his father's fine qualities, as well as great experience in modern statesmanship, having spent a decade first as Foreign Minister under his father's rule and then

The Waking Giant

Prime Minister before he finally became king. He is sophisticated and has many advanced ideas with regard to opening up of his country and distributing the country's assets more evenly.

Arabs, old-fashioned or sophisticated, not only have an innate sense of hospitality towards a guest in their own home or tent, they also take it for granted that any foreigner must be looked after; and shops have been shut, oases schoolchildren given a holiday, convoys held up indefinitely whilst some member acts as an unofficial guide to me. Here in Najran, Farouk Nabulsi, a Palestinian schoolteacher, sandwiched his classes between taking me around the oasis. Farouk was young and bulky and came from a well known Palestinian family who had owned large orange groves in Jaffa. With him I visited the hospital, the market where I changed Hadhrami money into Saudi Arabian riyals; and in the cool of the evening we went out to the gardens and fields on the outskirts of the town. The mud houses that rose above the walls were unpainted and solid, with rounded towers and the fields were sharply ridged for irrigation. On the brow of a hill were a group of neame trees. 'We call them "The Dancers",' said Farouk.

A huge crowd had gathered on a far field and we walked across the ridged beds which were ready for planting. Dancing was going on amongst the men and the women were chanting. The crowd was so dense it was impossible to see more than the heads of the dancers.

'What is it?' I asked a young man near me.

'It is a circumcision ceremony,' he said in good English, and then with mock despair, 'it is the *end*!'

The old crude methods of circumcision and the practice of waiting until the boy is quite old, is gradually dying out as are other customs. Even proof of virginity on the wedding night, it is rumoured, is not so strictly adhered to, though previously a girl would be killed by a brother or one of her male relatives to vindicate the family honour if such proof was not forthcoming.

Prince Khalid sent word that he would see me one late afternoon at his camp in the wadi. Farouk and I set off in the

Land-Rover. The wadi is wide here and very fertile and there is a plan afoot to build a great city not far from Ukhdud, the old Negrana Metropolis. And so history will repeat itself with the rebirth of one of the greatest cities on the Incense Route, for although there are indications that the route coming north went sometimes west through Beihan, Marib and the highlands of Yemen, and sometimes east as we had done, it always converged in the Najran Wadi.

The Emir's encampment is in ideal surroundings for the great community of tents is completely camouflaged by the thick foliage of bushes and trees. We pulled up near an extra large reception tent where two guards stood aside to allow us to enter. The tent was sixty feet long and lined with bright drapes and the ground was entirely covered with carpets. Chairs lined the wall space and a gold couch stood at one end. The rest of the tent was completely empty.

I slid out of my sandals at the opening, but Farouk being more sophisticated, left his shoes on. This habit borrowed from the Western world is unfortunate for now their beautiful carpets will become as dirty and worn as our own. We sat waiting on the chairs near the Emir's couch. My progress through the country depended on the good will of the man we were about to meet.

'Will he be difficult to talk to, Farouk?' I asked.

He shrugged. 'He is a soldier – and women . . . But perhaps you are different. Perhaps,' he repeated.

He was lolling in his chair when suddenly he made a lunge towards me with an agility that belied his bulk. With a sharp stamp of the foot he brought his shoe down fiercely on the carpet, missing my bare foot by inches. His face had lost its composure and he had gone quite white.

'What is the matter?' I asked. 'What is it?'

'It's . . .' he paused, looking for the word, 'it's . . . we call it an Egyptian spider.'

When he removed his foot there was a repulsive creature below it, more like a scorpion than a spider, with whitish transparent flesh, bulbous and altogether unpleasant. It was a particular species whose sting can cause almost instant death.

'It was going straight for your foot,' said Farouk, shaken.

The Waking Giant

'In the midst of life . . .!' I said as a slight man of medium height came into the tent.

Prince Khalid as Sudairi had the quick movements of a soldier; his face was long with an aquiline nose and a small military moustache. He greeted me in a friendly and relaxed manner and as one who was used to journalists, male and female. If the large general in the Yemen had been bored and impatient by inaction, it was nothing to this soldier's sense of frustration at having to reside here without the possibility of 'hitting back'. Already one thousand bombs and shells had been dropped within his territory and gas also had been used. The Prince has the singleness of purpose of a military man and he wished to speak of nothing else but the war; of Yemeni forced to fight Yemeni and of a country wrecked by a civil war that was motivated by outsiders. The constant threat on Saudi Arabian borders is a danger that tightens the intelligence and nerves making the country alert to the designs of outside nations. It is one of the lessons to be learnt by emerging countries, for wars, as we have seen, still exist although they are 'taboo', but they are becoming more and more protracted, eating into the countries involved while the natural procedure with its fighting, and gain or loss, through victory, has become diffused in multi-racial and biased talk. We spoke also of Arab nationalism which is not political or even military in the Arab character, but a feeling and a mystique of Arab unity – something the Westerner never understands or takes into account.

After coffee had been served from a beautiful coffee pot in tiny gold-rimmed handleless cups, and the traditional three cups of tea taken, the Prince sent for a large shell which had fallen but not exploded in the wadi. We traced the markings along the side; they were in Russian.

Nearly three hours had passed and we rose to go. The Prince stood up and smiled. '*Fi Aman Allah*,' he said as we went out into the cool night.

'He liked you,' said Farouk, 'it is good,' he added with satisfaction as we climbed into the Land-Rover.

The great ruined city of Ukhdud (Negrana Metropolis) lies farther out in the open wadi and away from present day

'It is Better to be Silent'

Najran. It covers an area of over twenty acres and the walled area alone extends for twelve acres. It was undoubtedly a wealthy and sophisticated city as the workmanship of the finely cut stones show. Many thick walls still stand and there are some excellent Himyaritic inscriptions, as well as some large mill wheels and a huge mortar lying on its side. I climbed to a high place with my secret Christian friend and it was possible to trace the outlines of the great city. It is not difficult to envisage its beauty for the setting is fine and surrounded by lines of grey hills. We thought of those other 10,000 Christians who had lived and been slaughtered here.

'It is better, even today, to be silent,' said my cautious friend.

After years of vandalism on the site the authorities now appreciate the importance of the ruins from an archaeological point of view and no unauthorized excavating is allowed. Many fine pieces were taken from the ruins and have now disappeared. There were vessels, jars, and jewellery in gold and silver as well as finely carved lintels. One bedu who found a beautiful bronze statue of a lion broke the head off to level the load in his camel bags. For many centuries the local people have been digging up the mixture of charcoal and bones which they use as fertilizer; bones of the Christians who were massacred no doubt!

It was decided that I would continue north with the pilgrims, which would be simpler than signalling to Jeddah, a suggestion which I quickly squashed. Hassan reappeared refreshed from the comforts and delights of Najran, but gloomy and wary of eye as ever.

'Beware of Mecca,' said my Christian friend, as we drank a last bottle of bogus beer, 'travelling in these fanatical areas – it's' – he struggled for the word – 'it is as you say, exceptional!'

10

Into the High Asir

A hunter went killing one day. As he carried on the slaughter, his eyes were streaming. Said one bird to another: 'Look at that man crying.' Said the other: 'Never mind his tears, watch his hands.'

— ARAB PROVERB

THE HAJJ has always brought business to the country and as the pilgrims pass through, people make money out of them. Along our route were huts to be used as overnight stops for pilgrims and many were in isolated places with either a small shop or improvised café near by. Near the few villages we passed small boys waited with sweets which they sold at high prices.

I had been given an open letter by Prince Khalid which had a magical effect each time it was presented. On leaving Najran we showed it at the same gate where we had met Ali, the Prince's Secretary, and the whole convoy was ushered through on the strength of it and after that Aytha, basking in the added prestige, kept it in his pocket. For a foreigner to travel alone without such a document would be almost impossible.

The area bordering on the Yemen was heavily patrolled for many miles and we were stopped several times. Just beyond the old well of al-Husayniyah in Wadi Habauna was a signpost which read: 'Riyadh 960 kilometres; Tathlich 290 kilometres.' The right fork led north-east to Wadi Dawasir and Jebel Tuwayq and on to Riyadh and we were taking the other which climbs to the highlands of Asir and Hijaz, passing through Hamdah, Tathlich, Bisha, Taif and Mecca. To the west of our track was the Tariq al-Fil – the Road of the Elephants – it passes through Abha the capital of Asir which lies seven thousand feet up in the mountains, and then the road continues north to join ours at Bisha. It was not only the road the Queen of Sheba used when she visited King Solomon but that taken by the Abyssinian king in his attempt to conquer Mecca in the sixth century A.D.

We climbed into the hills and ran along high depressions filled with fine alluvial dust which the pilgrim lorries had churned up. The vehicles stuck frequently and it was difficult to extricate them from the fine powder-like pockets. The high hills with their immediate dusty foliage have a strange ominous beauty, it is a grey-black country of huge granite boulders, an occasional slither of sand and shallow gulleys of green.

'Asir' means 'difficult' in Arabic and the rugged mountains are almost inaccessible rising to nine thousand feet. They fall sharply to the coastal plain of Tihama where there is an African influence, the people are darker and they live in conical huts similar to those seen in Ethiopia and along the East African coast. To the east, the mountains fall more gently towards the desert. Despite its ruggedness the slopes of the mountains form one of the most fertile areas in the country and it has a high population rate. Until recently there were few tracks and most of the transport was by donkey. During the monsoon in November and December these higher areas are often cut off completely. The people of Asir still watch the stars and the movement of Pleiades, for when it is low in the west the early rains are due; and Aldebaran coming low in the west at sunset, tells that ploughing is soon to commence. In the highlands the houses are made of stone and mud bricks, and because of the heavy rains, layers of slate, often twenty inches deep, protrude from the walls to prevent the water eroding them. The people have never been raiders for the mountain slopes produce in abundance all they need and in their orchards grow bananas, peaches, almonds and lemons. Many of them and especially the Rabi'a and Jahra tribes speak the the purist Arabic with a lilt that is pure poetry. Their hospitality is famous and it has been said that the host will offer both his bed and his wife to his guest.

My pilgrims were finding this part of the journey a slight anticlimax, for the danger had passed, but there were still many tough miles before they arrived in Mecca. We drove over rough ground, stopping occasionally to repair a puncture or to brew tea. These stops became more and more infrequent so that with barely a few hours rest, we were travelling day and night.

Hamaah in the Tathlich valley catered for pilgrims in a big way. A long line of open-faced huts could be hired for half a riyal apiece. In a larger hut two iron pots were set above charcoal fires, in one of them was a spicy stew and in the other water was boiling continuously. Around the café people sat on the ground or on benches beside a long table. The area around the huts was strewn with Coca-Cola bottles and caps, burst tyres, broken plastic bottles and discarded sandals. Pools of oil stained the ground and broken axles told of gross over-loading.

Business was slacking off, for most of the pilgrims had already passed through, although later they would return. Finally, however, when the last straggler had vanished, the place would be deserted – until the Hajj next year.

Around Hamdah are ruins and the remains of gardens now derelict. Mines were once in operation in the vicinity and the area formerly had a large population. The large and famous old tribe of Shammar came from these parts before they migrated to the north-east.

Hassan brought my thermos filled with hot water, pleased to be able to collect it direct from the café. His cold was slightly better and there had been a frightful and graphic description of the final results when the constipation cleared.

A little old man from Hauta in Hadhramaut had attached himself to me. He arrived during one of our stops to demand some Elastoplast for a cut on his finger, and had been invited to have a cup of Nescafé. Now it had become a ritual and every time we stopped he climbed into the Land-Rover and sat waiting expectantly.

'The Saudis are very fortunate,' he said, sipping his coffee noisily.

'Oh?'

'They had Abdul Aziz.'

'Which Abdul Aziz?'

Ibn Saud the Great Man

'The great one. He made this big country. He was greater than Ingrams.' Another loud sip. 'And he found oil.'

He was talking about His Majesty's father whom we call Ibn Saud. 'Yes,' I agreed, 'he was a very great man.'

'He should have made Hadhramaut his country. If he had not died . . .'

This was politics and controversial and a little surprising coming from an independent Hadhrami, so I let it pass.

As we were nearing Mecca the Moslems drew closer together; a common bond was uniting them and a singleness of purpose radiated from the groups, intangible and something of which they were probably quite unconscious. Would our own religion be stronger if we had such a pilgrimage? Christianity is divided within itself, although a lack of unity is a weakness of which we are often quick to accuse the Arab. Perhaps the restlessness and urge to travel which is so much part of our era would have a more productive goal if we had such a pilgrimage.

There were very few check-posts now and the way was easy to follow, for hundreds of tracks led in a general direction, sometimes splaying out over the ground or narrowing to one track if we came to a single defile. We stopped on a high wide plateau that sloped from the immediate horizon of granite rocks that were blackening as the sun sank behind them. With the dying of the lorries' engines it was still and quiet, as the pilgrims climbed down from the vehicles and formed an easy long line facing Mecca to perform the Salatu 'l Maghrib. The line stretched across the sand and wavered with a slightly forward movement, then foreheads touched the ground, and the only sound was the murmur of their leader. I moved behind them, for a Christian must never come between those in prayer and Mecca, and from a high rock watched the pilgrims, the only animated things in the vast landscape. At this moment thousands of pilgrims were turning towards Mecca in a similar way. If prayers are operative, as many think, what colossal strength lies in this ritual!

One incident shook the pilgrims as much as it did me for I am never proud of losing my temper. We had been driving since dawn with merely an hour's break and two hours sleep the previous night. I was tired and so was my back. Aytha, having stopped briefly to fill up with oil, was climbing back into his cabin when suddenly my temper snapped. I stood below him shaking with rage.

'This is infantile!' I said wrathfully. 'I am tired, *everyone* is tired! We have had little to eat since yesterday. This is nothing but a slave convoy. All of them . . .' indicating the dozens of startled faces looking down at me, '. . . need a proper meal. You can go on if you wish, but I am staying!'

The effect was electric. The *nasrani* who had been docile, who had caused so little trouble and had driven the 'Gazelle' across the sands and never stuck – was now acting like a bedevilled *jinn*!

Aytha, as startled as the rest, immediately called a halt of two hours for a meal, and the fresco of Arabs who had been mesmerized by my performance came slowly to life as they descended to the ground, still tense and quietened by my show of temperament. Hassan, woken from his doze, looked at me with startled eyes and slid out of the vehicle with a furtive air. Without a word or a martyred look he moved to the back of the Land-Rover and, extracting the thermos, went in search of hot water.

The old Hadhrami came and sat beside me, accepting without thanks but pleasantly, a mug of coffee and some biscuits. He had acquired a taste for the easily-made Nescafé.

'Soon we arrive in Bisha,' he said conversationally.

'When?'

'When?'

'Yes, how long will it take to arrive?'

'Four – five hours, *impkin*,' he said.

'That,' I said firmly, 'probably means eight or nine hours.'

He grinned. '*Impkin*,' he repeated. He sipped his coffee noisily. 'Bisha,' he informed me, 'is good place to find a wife.' He regarded me over the rim of the thermos mug quizzically and with a new light in his eyes. Since the outburst I had grown in stature even in his opinion, 'good wives from Bisha. But no,' he added with a slight air of regret, 'you do not need wife.'

To which I agreed.

We lost the lorries completely as, during the next seventy miles, we ran across the vast Bisha plain, a semi-fertile upland, riddled with lorry tracks. Now we saw lights other than those of the lorries – the first since Hadhramaut. Hassan woke occasionally and seeing a light indicated I change course to reach it. '*Camion*,' he would say authoritatively; but after obeying him twice and arriving at a bedouin encampment, I revolted.

'Go to sleep, Hassan,' I said, 'we are wasting too much petrol,' and I set off again to find the lorries.

Tiredness plays tricks on the eyes and mind. The tracks have a mesmerizing effect and there is an illusion of great over-hanging trees crowding in on the vehicle, even though one knows for certain that all around is a flat plain or desert. With the first light, the mystical trees recede, the world expands, and the open land lies all around.

Suddenly a low mud wall appeared to the right, running on and on, for we had arrived at Bisha. Hassan woke with a start as we reached a flat sealed road and the rattles and noises caused by the former rough ground suddenly stopped. The town slept and the roads were deserted. Low flat buildings, quite unadorned, lay all around. It was a low sprawling town clinging to the sand. The buildings formed streets and large squares and we were drawn to the only sign of activity as a flaring light came from a baker's oven. It stood in an open-fronted shop with a domed roof, and a young man was pushing large trays of dough inside. The flames threw quick shadows as they leapt at the high curved ceiling and white walls. The baker left the noisy oven and came to contemplate these odd arrivals from the plains. The police station, he assured us, was in the very next square and I, as a *nasrani*, must certainly go there.

We could see nothing of the lorries and drove to the police station which was the only two-storey building on the square. Its large iron doors were shut and bolted.

'That is all right,' I said to Hassan, 'we are outside the station. That is enough.' I turned off the car's engine and was asleep before he had time to answer.

The district of Bisha produces large quantities of dates which are sent all over the province, though little evidence of this could be seen in the flat dusty town. The wadi itself crosses the province from near the capital Abha and goes north-east until it converges with Wadi Dawasir. There is a great quantity of near-surface water which, although slightly brackish, is suitable for growing dates and here as in Wadi Tathlich there are signs of previous cultivation and of a much larger population than exists today. It is, however, growing again and being modernized. The new buildings for administration, schools, hospitals and agriculture are strictly utilitarian and the beautiful structures of previous times are being eclipsed or even demolished when they come in the path of planning.

At the police station I was allowed to use the bathroom; the large bowl of water and the privacy of a toilet were luxuries indeed. The officer made no attempt to look at my passport or inquire about my plans or destination and we drove off in search of the lorries.

It was a surprise to find that Aytha's mother lived here. His father, no doubt, being a merchant, had been travelling along this route for a long time. We were shown into a bare room with a few rugs but little else. It overlooked another square which was bare except for the only petrol pump in the town. Aytha's father had not been well during the journey. He had a haemorrhage. '*Cum un homra*,' he said with ironic humour. It was probably bilhartzia but the suggestion that he consult a doctor was not met with much enthusiasm. If doctors do not practise miracles at the first visit, the patient loses interest; the leather amulet worn round the neck, or even some of my pills seemed more effective.

We rested during the day, when it was hot, for we were all over-tired, and the town, devoid of greenery, was glaring and windy.

Towards late afternoon I ventured out and met a group of Palestinians; an engineer, a doctor, an agricultural specialist and a schoolteacher. They were on their way to a football match with the local boys. Here, as in Najran they were holding positions for which at the moment there were not enough educated Saudis.

We left the town at six in the evening but progress was slow for the lorries stuck often in the dust. In a particularly bad part Aytha motioned me to go on ahead. All around were flat churned-up beds of grey alluvial dust. I set off not sure which way to go and almost immediately the Land-Rover came to a sudden but definite halt as it sunk into the dust right up to the door. The two lorries coming after me, seeing my plight, pulled up. Without a moment's hesitation every male pilgrim climbed down from the lorries and came towards us, jumping through the sea of dust! There were far too many for all of them to touch the Land-Rover but those who could, took hold of the vehicle and with a mighty heave lifted it bodily up and to the left; first the rear and then the front. They repeated the procedure several times until at last the Land-Rover was on firm ground again.

'*Quais?*' they demanded cheerfully. '*Tamam?*'

'*Quais kathir!*' I said gratefully. '*Shukhran!*' and they turned happily towards the lorries again, all of them completely covered in dust, and made their way over the uneven ground.

Hassan, sitting beside me, nodded. '*Tamam,*' he affirmed. For it was the first time any of them had helped in a 'stick'.

At our next stop the old Hadhrami presented me with a bottle of orange squash; return hospitality for the many cups of Nescafé and biscuits he had shared with me. My mishap in sticking made me more approachable, more human to the pilgrims who came over to inquire how I was. The 'Gazelle' had seemed invincible to them previously, but now . . . If there was any more trouble, be assured they would be there. They would see the 'Gazelle' to Mecca!

'They make a fuss,' said the old man beside me when they had wandered off, for now he had a proprietary air towards me. 'Soon,' he continued, 'you are in Taif. After that, no more trouble.'

'I hear it is a beautiful town with cool air and many gardens?' I said.

He shook his head. 'Before, yes,' he said, 'but now – it is a city – *helas!*' He had the lotus-eating Hadhrami's scorn for the hustle and bustle of the twentieth century.

Before the introduction of air conditioning Taif had been the summer retreat of the inhabitants of Jeddah and as late as my previous visit it was a much coveted holiday place for those who were able to visit it.

It was almost midnight when I saw a glow on the horizon ahead.

'Hassan!' I said, 'what is that ahead?'

'Huh?'

'What is that glow on the horizon?'

'Taif,' he said, '*el hamdu lillah*,' and went to sleep again.

We drove down a neon-lighted double carriageway into a large unsightly town, chaotic with demolished buildings, half finished ones and large modern structures. The Taif of the beautiful gardens and leisurely way of life, mentioned by Philby and other travellers, seemed gone for ever. Aytha left his lorry on some recently cleared ground and climbing into the Land-Rover directed me towards the hotel. We drew up beside a plain square building in the main road; it was painted bright blue, with a large restaurant open to the pavement at one side. The few customers looked green under the brilliant neon lights. Aytha climbed out of the vehicle and taking my suitcase from the back, deposited it at the reception desk. He turned to me.

'Taif,' he said simply, and was gone.

The Forbidden City

I love him whose soul is deep even when wounded, and
who can perish even on account of a small affair; for he
gladly crosseth the bridge.   – F. NIETZCHE

I WOKE to the roar of traffic, and opening the shutters watched
the swiftly moving vehicles passing three and four abreast. The
wide double carriageway runs through the town leaving in
its wake few old buildings and ever-increasing modern ones
that toe the line with symmetrical efficiency. Some of them
were made of granite which is quarried in the vicinity and
these gave a certain solidarity. Street lighting of ultra modern
design hung like a silver thread down the centre and fabulous
limousines slid past the occasional cart or jeep.

The hotel had a narrow entrance hall with a high desk and a
small impersonal lounge near by. The stairs were wide and
tiled and the landings were bare. My bedroom was small and
sparsely furnished with a lumpy bed, a plain table and a
couple of dining chairs. A hard flat couch had brightly coloured
cotton cushions which were not very clean. In an outer
vestibule there was a shower and toilet which was shared with
the adjoining room. The toilet did not work and no water
came from the tap. It was obvious that ninety-nine per cent
of the clients were men.

Hassan appeared at ten o'clock with the Land-Rover. From
now on we would be on our own for Aytha was taking the
pilgrims direct to Mecca and I must skirt the Holy City to
reach Jeddah. The single vehicle would be more conspicuous
and the sooner I learned from my Embassy what the situation
was with regard to my driving the vehicle, the better. On my
previous visit as a royal guest, His Majesty gave me special

permission to drive across the country from east to west. This time I was in no such exalted position.

The traffic was noisy and very swift to our unaccustomed senses as we drove in search of the lorries. The pilgrims sat around in little groups intent on final preparations and they looked unfamiliar and vulnerable set against the bustling commercialism of the city. I found myself worrying about their cuts and boils, their headaches and the baby's rash. Would someone cope in the Holy City? Aytha was sitting on the ground ticking off the usual list. He put it aside and rose as we came up. I tried to say 'thank you', but nothing could express or repay his help and kindness. It had been an intuitive, almost unspoken friendship and, on his part, generously given with no thought of reward of any kind; and it was doubtful if we would ever meet again.

As I climbed back into the Land-Rover the little Hadhrami came up.

'Come back to Hadhramaut!' he said gaily. 'Bring the "gazelle" and we will make a journey! *Fi aman allah.*'

We stopped to ask the direction out of town and a young Palestinian pushed his way through the crowd.

'To Jeddah? You cannot drive to Jeddah! The road runs through Mecca,' he said. 'Christians fly direct from here and arrange for a driver to take the vehicle through the city' – he suddenly realized that I was driving. 'In any case, women cannot drive in this country.'

I thanked him quickly, glad we were speaking English and drove off. So that was that! The more sophisticated people knew about this law. However, so long as Hassan was with me I was not so conspicuous, for in this country, as they drove on the right, the driver's seat was on the left where he sat.

The air was pleasant and clear, for Taif lies over five thousand feet above sea level. It was one of the oldest and loveliest towns in the Hijaz and the Prophet Mahammad stayed here for some time. Though it is not a holy city similar to Mecca and Medina, until quite recently it was necessary for non-Moslem to have special permission to enter the town.

The road towards Mecca had long stretches of good tarmac surface and there was an air of bustle, of building and construc-

Sail

tion far out into the bare uplands. Finally the ground began to break up into smaller hillocks where more vegetation grew and I recognized Sail, a small village which is a junction of caravan routes from Mecca, Najd and the south, for I had passed it on my way from Riyadh previously. The village stands on a miniature platform surrounded by gulleys and sharp little hills. It is one of the stations where pilgrims change into the *ihrâm*, and little huts spread along the crest of the hill. Most of the pilgrims had already changed and we were surrounded by a sea of spotlessly white figures. The *ihrâm* consists of two pieces of cloth which have no fastenings or seams. One is worn around the hips and the other over the shoulders leaving the right arm bare. All pilgrims are bare headed although it is permitted to carry an umbrella and to wear loose slippers. From now on they will wear these clothes until the rites are completed. Most of the women wear large enveloping garments with two slits for the eyes, although their costumes change with their nationality. It is necessary however for all women to bare their faces in front of the Kaaba.

We were not noticed as we slid past the crowded police station and edged our way through the white crowd. It would be impossible to tell which of these figures were bedu, millionaires or royalty.

Out of Sail there is a long and gradual descent towards Wadi al Yamaniyah which runs towards Mecca. This long hill is covered with a deep layer of snow-white sand so that it looks like a ski-run and the lorries sped past us like great outsized ski-ers.

Previously the base of Wadi al Yamaniyah had been a torrent bed of large boulders over which I had been forced to travel at about eight miles an hour. Now a rough levelled-out road had been constructed which was already badly corrugated by the heavy traffic, but by driving at full speed to guard against skidding, progress was certainly faster. The wadi narrowed to about three hundred yards and the hills each side rose to over two thousand feet. I looked in vain as we passed for the huge rock known as 'The Nomad's Tomb' which, legend has it, fell from the cliff crushing a bedu who was fleeing from Mecca having stolen from the Great Mosque.

The Forbidden City

Had progress in the shape of the new road taken that unquiet spirit's grave and monument away?

The wadi widens again and forms a basin where Wadi Yamaniyah and Wadi Lîmûn meet. Near by is the site of ancient Okâz where in pre-Islamic times an annual fair was held. The great Arabian poets, Al Aashâ, El Hârith, ibn Halliza, Amr-ul Qais and Tarafa bin El Abd came to recite their poems. Subsequently the poems were set out in gold lettering and hung in the Kaaba in Mecca and such was the worship of the eloquence of words that the Arabs bowed down before them.

A spring of sweet water comes from the south cliff at Saima and the little community is set around it. In the gardens near by grow dates, limes, oranges, lemons and bananas, as well as millet and barley. Two large stalls stood in the shade of the palms where fruit and vegetables made a magnificent display. A tiny mosque hugs the cliff side and a small police station stands near by. It looked green and lush and there was a pleasant holiday air, and yet here in Saima, Doughty was nearly murdered when he passed through the village on his way to Jeddah. Had he died it would have been just another infidel to the bedouin, but what a loss, both to us and Arabia had Doughty's epic never been written!

Remembering the difficulty I had experienced in trying to by-pass Mecca previously, I stopped for information, and immediately most of the inhabitants, as well as many passing pilgrims, were giving advice and instructions. A police officer wandered over, saw nothing amiss in my driving the Land-Rover and assured us there was no difficulty whatsoever and we could 'not go wrong'.

We left the track and crossed to the north side of the wadi towards Wadi Lîmûn. This would be a wider detour missing the ancient well of Jarana with its Kufic inscriptions and the tomb of Maimuna, the twelfth and last wife of the Prophet; she had been married here and asked to be buried here also.

We became involved in a labyrinth of sandy hillocks and had lost all sign of a track when we came to a house set up against the far cliff. Hassan went in search of some direction. He was worried at being so near the Holy City with me and was visibly relieved when the young owner of the house offered to take us round – for sixty riyals.

We continued along the wadi towards Salah and Akar looking for a track and for two hours we doubled back amongst the sharp little hills that surround Mecca. When the valleys opened out there were viaducts and bunds to catch the water and silt which helped to supply Mecca with fertile ground as well as water. Queen Zubaida, the wife of Baghdad's Caliph Harun al Rashid, paid for the construction of water tunnels to supply the city and a rock tunnel was built from the spring of Ain Zubaida nine miles south of Mecca. This devout person was also responsible for the sinking of wells and the construction of cisterns to catch rain water along the entire pilgrim route from Baghdad to Mecca.

The narrow peaked hills that surround Mecca gave an oppressive effect as we drove along the narrow defiles. In one of these passes the Abyssinian Christian King Abraha advanced from Sana in Yemen when he came to seek vengeance on the Meccans who had desecrated the Cathedral in Sana, because it was drawing more pilgrims than the heathen shrines of Mecca. King Abraha with his large army and many elephants arrived so far and the Meccans in a last desperate effort to stay the advancing army, ambushed them in a narrow pass, hurling rocks and stones from the hills around. Even the swallows, legend has it, dropped pebbles on the invaders who, taken by surprise, were forced to retreat with heavy losses.

We came finally to Jamoun, an old well surrounded by an irrigation system which has been used for over two thousand years. The water lies near the surface and the ground is lowered and a complicated system of walls and irrigation channels, which lets the water out over the lowered ground, is used. This area now has a commercial air with fine roads and factories, the gardens have been abandoned and many of the palms are dying for want of attention.

We stopped when we came to the main Jeddah to Mecca road and our elegant guide left us, immediately hitching a lift back through the Holy City. Ahead of us lay forty miles of fine tarmac road, crowded with fast-moving traffic which increased as we entered Jeddah. Large establishments in bizarre colours lined the roads, giving place to shops, super-markets and modern blocks of flats. Here, as in Taif, large construction programmes made it necessary to pick our way over broken ground along the Avenue Abdul Aziz and the Midan Malik. Vehicles came towards us from every direction, but there was a pleasant air of goodwill amongst the slightly erratic and exotic drivers who managed their luxurious limou-ines with expertise.

I paid Hassan and said good-bye with little regret and he set off immediately for Hadhrami friends who lived in the Suk. The British Embassy, true to its reputation for hospitality, lent me an apartment in the Embassy compound, which was as well for hotel rooms at this moment of Hajj fever were fetching as much as £35 per night!

12

Jeddah – of Frankish Consuls

Adopt the pace of nature; her secret is patience.
— EMERSON

SAUDI ARABIA and especially Jeddah is not the best place for
journalists who generally have little time to spare. There are
endless tales of long waits, confusion, confiscation of cameras
and other property, and of wasted journeys. However their
tormentors act in high good humour and with charm, assuring
them that with patience all will be finally well. To add to the
journalists' confusion, and any others to whom time is important,
is the fact that Saudi Arabia has *four* times; and you can take
your pick. There is ordinary standard or G.M.T. plus the
three or four hours necessary for longitude and this is used in
the oil industry base at Dhahran and in Jeddah. There is also
the Dhahran time used by the oil company Aramco which
adds an hour for daylight during the summer months and is
sometimes used in Jeddah as well. The third is Moslem sun
time which makes midnight at the time of sunset – and
naturally changes with the sun. It is used in Riyadh and all
government offices; this throws one out six hours. Finally the
foreigners use what is known as European Local Time when
they set their watches six hours behind the Moslem Sun Time,
whatever that happens to be. Wits will tell you there is a fifth –
A.M.T. or Arab-*marleesh*-time!

Some day Jeddah may be a fine city though at the moment
one grieves at the ruthless destruction of the old houses for
which the city was famous, and off the main streets an occasional house of the old style still survives with its ornate carved
and enclosed balconies, shaded by an incredibly tall neame
tree. But it is probably a house waiting for its old occupant to
die so that the younger generation can pull it down.

Jeddah – of Frankish Consuls

The veneer of modern Jeddah has gone deeper now; it has become cosmopolitan with the anonymity of a large city. Previously life centred round a few prominent personalities, as well as the Royal Princes and the Finance Minister; but today they are lost in the growth of commercialism.

Surprisingly in the chaos of rebuilding, the site of Eve's Tomb still remains. It is a mound forty-five feet long enclosed in a high wall where Eve is reputed to be buried. Gone, however, and without trace, is the Green Palace of Ibn Saud, the present king's father. It was little more than a wooden house with a small *maglis* and a raised wooden platform, and through its corridors, it was said, went the ghost of a young wife who had committed suicide here.

The Kandara Palace Hotel is still the main meeting place for the young men of Jeddah and the best hotel in the town. Several luxury chalets have been erected in the garden as well as a fine modern swimming pool with dressing-rooms and showers for both men and women. There are several new hotels as well, and the bizarre structures that were a feature of the new Jeddah are toning down.

It was nearing the time for the pilgrims' departure for Mecca and still they arrived; there was a plane every ten minutes and the population of Jeddah more than doubled before they left. Barracks built by the Ministry of Pilgrimage at the airport and the docks were full to overflowing and many ships, after disgorging their passengers, stood by in the harbour, ringed with festive lights and awaited the pilgrims' return. On reclaimed land by the waterfront near the city centre dozens of huge lorries were parked and their passengers camped alongside. As well as the interchange of goods, especially carpets, the kiosks and small carts sold fruit, drinks and ice-cream. The lorries were gay with ornately decorated iron guards and bright tassels and flags. The drivers displayed their vehicles, fine Mercedes Benz, Volvo, Bedford and Leyland with obvious pride, and chatted about their journey. They had come from as far away as Iran, Turkey and Pakistan. If I should want to return with them, they could always make an extra place.

Suddenly, spontaneously, the final pilgrimage began and

Performing the Hajj

Jeddah, within the space of hours was deserted. The airport was empty and the docks closed. Not one lorry stood on the reclaimed ground near the waterfront, nor a Coca-Cola cart, and around the shut kiosks a couple of dogs nosed through the debris. For the rest of Jeddah it was a three-days' holiday and most shops and offices closed their doors. The remaining inhabitants went to the beaches or flew to the cool hills around Taif.

The sacred precincts of Mecca extend roughly fifteen miles from the city centre and there are signposts on all the main roads warning non-Moslems to go no farther. The grand Haran Mosque is Islam's holiest shrine and all who enter Mecca go there immediately to pray. Here also the ceremony of the performing of the Hajj begins. Having washed and removed his sandals the pilgrim enters the galleries and passes through the Mosque's enormous outer galleries, a new section which covers an area of fifteen acres and was built at a cost of roughly £40,000,000. Prayers are recited here and four prostrations performed in thanks for having reached the Holy spot. From here the pilgrim catches sight of the Kaaba beyond, which rises above a sea of white moving figures; it is made of Meccan granite and is draped in black. This is the stone that Moslems face five times a day, to pray, no matter where they are. The original Kaaba was destroyed centuries ago and is believed to have been rebuilt by Abraham and his son Ismael. Before the coming of Islam, it was the most important of three hundred and sixty sacred idols in Mecca to which men and women made the pilgrimage, then, however, it was necessary to appear completely nude for they believed their sins could be thrown off with their clothes. Today the pilgrim, dressed in traditional *ihrâm*, prays before the Kaaba and if possible touches the stone with his right hand or kisses it. Now begins the *Towaf* or walk round the Kaaba, always keeping the building on the left. It is encircled seven times, the first three at a quick trot if the crowds permit, in imitation of the Prophet who ran to prove to his enemies who were spreading rumours of his illness, that this was not so. Each circuit is accompanied by prayers, recited in a low voice; and there is a prayer for different parts of the building. At the black stone, set in silver which stands at the eastern corner, the pilgrim raises his hands and cries: '*Allaahu Akbar!*' (God is great). A deep murmur comes from the crowd as it moves and at El Metzem, the section between the Black Stone and the door of the building, he presses against the wall asking Allah to pardon his sins.

Forty feet from the Kaaba is Mekam Ibrahim, which consists of six small pillars supporting a domed roof that covers the stone called El Hajar al Asad where Abraham stood and left his footprint when he was rebuilding the Kaaba. After praying here the pilgrim moves to the left of the stone of Zemzem where he drinks the miraculous waters believed to cure most illnesses and, if possible, washes.

Now it is decreed the pilgrims run between the two little hills of Szafa and Marwa this is called the *Say*. This is now enclosed in the precincts of the great mosque and the journey should be performed seven times, with a prayer at each end and finishing at Marwa. According to Moslem tradition Abraham left Madjer here with the baby Ismael and she ran desperately between the two hills looking for water for the baby. The Angel Gabriel appeared and, seeing her plight, struck the ground with his foot which brought forth the spring that now feeds the well of Zemzem.

All is still after the sunset prayers when the circling stops, and the scene moves to the plain of Arafat fourteen miles away where the next day the great gathering of the Hajj takes place. The plain is a fabulous sight with thousands of tents, large umbrellas and families camping, resting and praying. At sunset a cannon is fired as a signal for the departure to Mina and the great exodus begins. It is becoming more and more chaotic as every kind of transport, trucks, limousines, animals and the people travelling by foot, jostle each other. Soldiers in *ihrâm* try to keep order and any wrong-doer is harshly dealt with. The journey of roughly six miles may take many hours.

On the outskirts of Mina is a stone buttress or pillar, one of three, where, it is said, the devil tried to tempt Abraham when he prepared to sacrifice his son to God. But God substituted a ram on finding Abraham could not be tempted. The pilgrims throw seven stones to stave off the devil and slaughter an animal to commemorate Abraham's offering.

Except for the days of the Hajj, Mina remains almost empty during the year, but now with its pilgrim huts and cafés there is scarcely room to walk. A room shared with three or four others can cost £30 and most people must camp in the streets. Throughout the day at the official slaughterhouse on the outskirts of the town pilgrims slit the throats of animals, and thousands of sheep, cows and camels are killed in offering and then distributed to the poor. Each year the amount of slaughtered animals grows and great piles are left to rot; this is tempered only by the fact that – miracle-like – it *always* rains on the following day and so washes the carcasses and ground around.

Suddenly on the second day Mina blossoms when the pilgrims change into everyday clothes; and all the beautiful colours of Africa and the East turn the dim crowded town into a fairyland. There is joy everywhere for they have completed the Hajj!

To some this is not the final climax for they will make the three-hundred-mile journey north to Medina, the second Holy City where Mahammad spent the last ten years of his life. But the others turn their faces towards Jeddah and think of the quickest means of returning to their homes.

As swiftly as they had departed the pilgrims returned; many of the lorries passed through without delay and the docks and airport seethed again, as there was a scramble to secure transport. Others stayed a while and the city was colourful with the many national costumes. The Hajji window-gazed at the modern shops and thronged the old covered suk where everything from jewellery to spices can be bought.

One evening I turned from the covered way into a smaller street of local cafés; most of them had a raised platform and were open to the street. On one of these raised portions was a figure, slightly familiar, in a long white dishdasher and cap. He rose as I approached.

'Memsahib?'

'Mubarak! What are you doing in Jeddah? And how smart you look!'

'I come for Hajj,' he said, giving me one of his toothless grins. 'I come by ship.'

'And now you are just back from Mecca. With your family?'

His face fell. 'No,' he said dispiritedly.

'They are still in Mukalla?' I asked, but he shook his head.

It was difficult to piece the story together but when he returned to Mukalla his wife and son had already gone. He now had the hopeless task of finding them in the crowded city.

'Will you go back to Mukalla?' I asked.

'Yes – back to Mukalla.' The uncertainty and probable loss of his small son had cured him at last of his wanderlust.

'How was the Hajj?' I asked.

'Terrible, memsahib,' he said, 'no room, no room at all. The people! And the traffic! This year it is worse, the cars worse than ever. You would not believe . . .'

But I believed – traffic, it seems, is a problem with all races and creeds.

On such a journey it is well to know the moment to assert oneself or when it is politic to stay in the background and cause as little comment as possible. From the administration point of view I went warily; to ask permission to continue north could stir up all sorts of trouble and queries. Before me was a pamphlet of information to visitors to Saudi Arabia. A permit to include the vehicle, I read, should be obtained from the Minister of the Interior before entering the country. Carnets for the vehicle were not recognized nor was an International Driving Licence. It was therefore necessary to procure a Saudi licence which cost twenty-seven riyals and could take up to two months. As the carnet was not recognized, a customs deposit could be demanded; and finally, two vehicles must always travel together. I read on to find that the journey I had just taken from Aden was: 'Not possible!'

My own Embassy arranged for an exit permit and left it at that. The few ministries I contacted took as their cue my assumption that the situation was normal and any information I wanted was given easily and promptly; but I was in no hurry and with the contrariness of human nature, things came easier and quicker for me.

I was handicapped by not having transport, for women definitely did not drive in Saudi Arabia. In Jeddah this was a great inconvenience to the Western women for it is a sprawling city and there is little public transport which they can use. If a woman is caught driving a vehicle it is her husband who takes the rap and I, in the circumstances, would have been an embarrassment. The Ministry of Information therefore instructed Abdul Abbas to escort me and help wherever possible. He was a good-looking young man, immaculate in white robe and kuffiyah, who drove a large American limousine with great efficiency.

We drove one afternoon along the river estuary where the inhabitants of Jeddah go to bathe. Some parts of the waterfront are bought by wealthy people or by the various embassies who erect a high wall enclosing huts; but other reaches are open to the general public. We stopped on the flat sandy water's edge alongside other parked cars carrying veiled women and their children. A jeep drew up beside us driven by a young man whose wife and two sisters were all unveiled. They were gay and happy, if a little self-conscious at their precocious behaviour. The husband had been working abroad and his wife was now accustomed to the freer life. I chatted with them but Abbas stayed away, for even modern behaviour does not allow a man to speak to a nice unattached Saudi girl!

Many modern Saudis marry the more sophisticated Lebanese and Palestinian girls which probably works better than marriages with those of European or American nationality, for with the latter the contrast is too great from their own women who are just emerging from purdah. Officially the emancipation of the Saudi woman is now encouraged and the next decade should see them in a very different position. Already many of the local women move about more, they belong to the International Women's Club whose members meet at the various embassies or at a merchant's house. On these occasions the Saudi women arrive completely veiled, but once in the house they remove their outer garments to reveal modern clothes that would be the envy of most Europeans.

These women are poised and intelligent and if they have a go-ahead husband they often travel with him unveiled to Beirut, the U.S.A. or Europe. Some young women have been educated at universities abroad and are now helping in the new emancipation. One attractive young woman, the sister of one of the radio interviewers, took her B.A. in philosophy, psychology and sociology at Alexandria University. Now she is Assistant Supervisor of Women's Activities in the Ministry of Social Affairs and played a large part in the establishing of the Co-operative Society of Women's handicrafts. She showed me over the society's quarters where there was a display of work. Each member buys shares and attends classes in which she can learn dressmaking or other crafts. There were modern clothes which she showed me with pride.

'It is exciting for them to find they are clever with their hands, and what is more,' she added with a laugh, 'it brings them out of the house!'

The social life of Jeddah is a polyglot affair with the sophistic-ated Saudis mixing with the Europeans with ease. There is a lot of bathing along the river and parties where glasses are juggled between drinkers and non-drinkers, and much enter-taining in the home, for servants, although expensive, are plentiful; and there are restaurants, Arab and European, to suit all purses.

Slowly I gathered information about the route north towards Medina which would have to be by-passed. There are two routes from then on to the Jordan border; along the Hijaz Railway or the new road which runs parallel with it but to the east. The latter passes the ancient Jewish settlement of Khaibar, Taima, and joins the railway at Tabuk, four hundred and fifty miles north of Medina. The Hijaz railway follows the Incense Route for most of the way and the same track was used by pilgrims before the railway was built. There was little information about the possibility of following the railway which had been wrecked and completely put out of action during the First World War. As well as being along the old route, it passes through Madain Salih, the Nabataean City of Rock Tombs which rivals and is far more remote than Petra in Jordan. Many early travellers tried without success to reach the

In Search of Aisha

city but Doughty succeeded and has left a classic and vivid description of it. Without a doubt it was one of the important cities on the route taking its place with Shabwa, Marib, Najran and Petra. Searching for someone who had taken the journey led me automatically to the French Embassy, for where there are Frenchmen there will be archaeologists, professional or amateur. I had met the Cultural Attaché in the Fezzan, Libya, years before and he sent me to the Jordanian Embassy where two men had returned from their own country along this route.

'You would not be able to go alone,' said the First Secretary, 'and in any case you would miss many of the tombs and inscriptions. Madain Salih is in a much wider, more open valley than Petra. There is a party from the American Embassy planning a trip; why not go and see them?'

The American Embassy compound lies four miles out of the city centre. It is a pleasant modern and low-lying building and I was passed from one air-conditioned room to another until in the First Secretary's office, Slater Blackistan confirmed that they were making the trip. He was a tall, quietly spoken man with an assured manner, and with him was Brooks Wrampelmeier, also of the Embassy. He was very fair and Teutonic looking.

'Yes,' confirmed Slater, 'we are trying to incorporate a visit to Madain Salih in a trip to the north-east. The Spanish Ambassador and a member of the Agricultural Department are coming also. We would be delighted to have you along.'

It was as easy as that.

Finally I went in search of Aisha, a young friend of my previous visit, but found a large block of apartments and offices standing on the site of the family's beautiful home. Aisha, I found out, has since married a wealthy Kuwaiti, and flown. She had been a great worry and source of disappointment to her family for she was a rebel, independent and worst of all – thin! She would never, they confirmed, find a husband being only half a woman. But Aisha had moved with lithe grace up the great staircase, laughing and unconcerned – and now? Perhaps, after all, she was merely ahead of her own time.

13

The Hijaz Railway

'Kul Wàhed aly Dín-Hu'

THE LOW bungalow set on rocky ground beside the electricity power station, faced the main road on the outskirts of Medina. This was as far as any Christian could go and Charles Dutton, a Scot, had been in charge of the plant for several years. He had naturally never been into the Holy City though with the help of a staff of twenty-five he supplied the town with its electricity. All his provisions, goods, mail and spares were brought from the city by one of his Moslem staff. His second-in-command was Khalid Khurdi who, although born in Saudi Arabia, had a Kurd father. This is a common way of naming people in the country and one often meets a person with the name 'Yemeni' or 'Hadhrami' whose family came from those countries. Lutfi, the storekeeper, was from Gaza, and a tall young man named Talal was an apprentice electrician. A little old man whose duties included being gatekeeper, tea maker and listening for the telephone bell, had a familiarity of manner and gait which was explained when he said he came from Hadhramaut. There is an impartiality and common-sense attitude about Scots which makes them the best people to work in foreign countries; and they have the same attitude towards hospitality so that I did not feel I disrupted his household as I waited a couple of days for the appearance of my party from Jeddah.

My last night in Jeddah had been spent with Aprille and Slater Blackistan at their house in the American Embassy compound. The members of our small expedition and their wives came to dinner. There was Slater and Brooks Wrampelmeier; His Excellency German de Caso Ridaura the Spanish Ambassador, and Riad Stambouli an executive of the

Medina

Agricultural Department. The party had the ease and slickness one associates with American hostesses; life running on very smooth wheels. Very early next morning Aprille saw me off, for now that I was alone in the Land-Rover it was safer to be away from Jeddah before there were many people about. As I drove through the gates of the compound I glanced back at Aprille standing on the steps looking fresh and elegant and then caught sight of myself in the car's mirror, at my far from *soignée* hair-do and my freckled nose and with all the travel-stained mementoes around me, a pair of tiny Greek slippers hanging from the mirror, the policeman's truncheon, St. Christopher and the printed 23rd Psalm pasted on the dash-board; the things that make up so much of my life. I sighed, I was certainly no successful hostess, wife and mother, but perhaps it does take all sorts to make a world!

An excellent road runs for three hundred miles from Jeddah to Medina and it follows the coast through barren, uninhabited country. Ninety-six miles from Jeddah is Rabigh with a petrol station and a restaurant known for the excellence of the fish caught locally. The small harbour near by was used during the First World War when supplies were landed for Lawrence and his men. From here the road runs north-east through low hills until a signpost instructs Christians to take heed, for the boundary limits of Medina are in sight.

Legend has it that on arriving in Medina the Prophet let his camel wander at will, and at the spot where it stopped and knelt, he chose to build his first place of worship. Within its enclosure is the Holy Tomb. The mosque is reputed to be beautiful in its simplicity and the graceful minaret can be seen from the hills beyond. This was the city in which the Prophet rose to power and during the twelve years he spent here before he died, Islam had spread to Spain and Morocco in the west and India in the east.

My party arrived in a Long-wheel-base Land-Rover, and a 'pick-up'. They looked immaculate and prepared for any eventuality. Slater and Brooks took it in turn to drive the Land-Rover, and Ali, a driver from the U.S.A. Embassy, managed the 'pick-up'. His Excellency, a slight-built man with a mercurial manner and much charm, came with me.

The Hijaz Railway

'Some day, perhaps,' he said, 'I shall make a journey such as yours and so I shall learn from you how to drive in difficult country.'

Riad, the agricultural expert, was a warm little man who should not have been making such a tough journey for, despite a weak heart, he worried and coped with anything that arose.

We filled our tanks at the petrol station just outside the Medina boundaries and leaving the road cut off to the left to by-pass the city. The detour is not as difficult nor so extensive as that around Mecca, and Jebel al Jimmal, which separated us from the town, had a track along its base. We drove over a low shoulder of the Jebel and before us lay the straight line of the Hijaz Railway, running north from the city towards the hills. Ahead were farms with cultivated fields and to the right was Sultana, the district and palace of the king, which was set behind a wall; beyond in the city rose the beautiful slender minaret of the mosque, blue-grey, and bringing, in some odd way, the city that much nearer.

The railway, which has been out of commission since it was wrecked by Lawrence and the Arabs during the First World War, is now being repaired. There is a strange mystique about railways and the various schemes put forth for their construction across the most remote and unlikely regions of the earth are legend. Here in Arabia the idea of building a railroad to transport pilgrims to the Holy Cities was contemplated as far back as 1864. Again in 1869 with the opening of the Suez Canal the project was reconsidered as a more business-like proposition by the Germans to counteract the British advantage of the canal. It was part of a plan to assist the Turkish Empire to set up a series of railroads over their many Middle East territories; the Germans envisaged a railroad to Medina and Mecca which would finally run the length of the peninsula to the southern coast of Arabia, much as the Incense Route had done. The Turks would have the added advantage of being able to garrison this part of Arabia, and the work was started at the end of the last century. From the beginning there were difficulties with the local bedu who were jealous of the threat to their caravan trade and the profits they made out of the

Rebuilding the Railway

pilgrims. They not only harassed the construction but refused to work on the project, therefore five thousand Turkish soldiers were brought in to do the work and to keep order. Musil in 1912 speaks of the soldiers on the railway still having to repair damage done by the hostile bedouin. Blockhouse stations were set up every twelve or fifteen miles as an added precaution. Messner, the German engineer, was in charge, and the project which was to become a great engineering feat, is mainly due to him. The railway from Damascus to Medina, a distance of eight hundred miles, was opened in 1908, though the further construction of the rail to Mecca was never even started and ten years after the opening, the railway had been put out of action, by Lawrence and his men. During the final months of the campaign the allies repaired the northern end of the railway from Ma'an to Damascus as they advanced towards the city, and this section has remained open for a skeleton service ever since.

For many years now the question of rebuilding or repairing the railway has been studied by a committee set up for the purpose. It consisted of twelve members, three each from Jordan, Syria and Saudi Arabia, and each country agreeing to pay a third of the money required. After several surveys the contract was finally given jointly to two British firms, and work was started in 1964. This time the motivation for its construction was almost entirely religious. The delays and complications, including financial ones, has affected the completion of the work which was scheduled for 1966 and the original estimate of eight million pounds may well reach double that amount. The advisability of the whole project is the cause of endless discussion, especially as the Saudis have an excellent road from Jeddah through Medina to the Jordan border, and it is surmised that the trains will be used only once a year during the Hajj. But will this be so? Will this line of communication, together with the road, not open up the sparsely populated part of Arabia through which it passes and also make the unique site of Madain Salih extremely accessible? Thousands of tourists visit the sister city Petra in Jordan each year, now they will be able to continue south with great ease. The tourist and his camera may be ridiculed but he does much

137

towards creating understanding and breaking down prejudice and fear.

We turned north beside the railway line, following faint tracks left by the construction engineers. The sleepers had been removed and stacked in piles. They were made of iron, for wooden ones would be taken by the bedu almost before they were laid. Some were stamped by the German engineers and dated 1907. The surface to take the tracks has been levelled and many low viaducts of granite blocks were still in excellent condition, while others had already been repaired. It was grey, dusty country with sweeping hills covered with straggling bushes. After seven miles Makhit, the first station out of Medina, lay below us in a shallow hollow. It was surrounded by the low hills and as we drove towards the deserted group of buildings a bleak and lonely atmosphere came out to meet us and there was an odd sense of tragedy in the grey still scene.

On each side of the track was a building and a small sharp mound beyond had a hastily erected pill-box on its summit. The blockhouse below was made of granite blocks and high stone steps led into an open courtyard with rooms each side. Directly opposite, stone steps led to a gallery above. Beside the steps a rough platform used as a fireplace had blackened walls which was the only clue that there had been any habitation here, for everything removable had long since gone. High in the walls were slits for rifles. The building opposite was smaller with a series of arches and a place for offices, built of the same granite blocks. There was no platform and the rail tracks disappeared between a cut in the grey hills ahead.

We followed the rail as it continued along the western slopes of Jebel al Rayda and the Wadi Hamd, which is called after the bush that grows in abundance along its base. This great wadi starts south-east of Medina and runs north, changing its name to Issl before finally reaching the Red Sea south of Waqh. There is no doubt that a route north from Taif joined this wadi having by-passed Mecca in the days before that city was a place of pilgrimage. Formerly this area was a great hunting ground and quantities of ibex, leopard, oryx and ostrich could be found, but now even the oryx has become quite rare.

Antara, the Hero-poet

After a few miles we were forced to leave the tracks and cut up into the hills; below us was the station of Tafira, solitary as the previous one had been.

The railway, following the old route passes ancient wells and reservoirs, and there are traces of communities that had flourished at one time. This is the country of the hero-poet Antara, a man-God of great stature and composer of one of the seven Golden Arab songs. The bedu say that on the mountain-top near Istabi Antar there is a manger and rings of stone, 'Where the hero's mare stood bound'.

Now there are no settlements and the few people we saw were nomads moving with their camels and goats. Occasionally we caught sight of a fox but there were few birds and even the little thorb is rare and more difficult to discern in the wadis than on the bare jol. This lizard with its wide flat body is considered a delicacy and is roasted whole in cinders. I have often rescued one and kept it as a pet, for they became tame and docile when fed on small leaves and insects.

We passed a small working party of Yemeni who are employed as stone workers here as they are in southern Arabia. They were working energetically and with a cheerfulness generally found with these pleasant people. Near by were a couple of flat-cars which had been thrown by explosion on their sides and away from the track, only the shell remained for everything portable had been removed.

A few miles on was the advance camp of the sub-contractors. Their quarters were luxurious with air-conditioned caravans, used as kitchen, bedrooms and bathroom. There was a large open tent for meals. Rumours that work was about to be suspended owing to lack of funds was dispelled by this busy camp. There were two geologists and a surveyor. They invited us into the tent for coffee. One of the geologists turned to me.

'Toy? Are you Barbara Toy?' I nodded. 'Well! We heard you last night on the radio from Jeddah, you were the guest on "My Kind of Music".' He laughed. 'You certainly travel fast!'

The next section of the rail runs through extremely rough country. The men spoke of old ammunition found near the viaducts and of the caution necessary in dealing with the whole area. Many believe that somewhere along the line there is a great horde of Turkish gold which was abandoned and buried by the retreating army during the war. The men were dubious about the advisability of us continuing up this section of the line.

'You can, I suppose,' said the surveyor, 'but the next section really is tricky and not of much interest. Better you go back to the main road near Khaibar – which is worth seeing – and thirty miles north of the town. Turn off again and rejoin the railway south of Madain Salih.'

We took their advice and retraced our steps some way, joining the main road near Uhud on whose summit, it is claimed, Aaron is buried. We were now skirting the eastern slopes of Jebel al Baidha which rose in a blue haze to the left, and we passed Medina's airport on our right. The last of the pilgrims had departed but it still bore witness of their presence for litter was being cleared in the café where we were served sandwiches and orange squash by two extremely tired little men.

The road now runs into the great volcanic tract of Harrat al Khaibar, a wilderness dreaded by early travellers. The landscape becomes entirely black with peaks, cones and the craters of volcanoes. At the turn of the century one volcano erupted with such violence that the glow was seen as far north as Ma'an, five hundred miles away. To the east is Jebel al Abyadh (White Mountain) which, although black, gives a white appearance when the fierce sun shines on it. Near the road is the ancient dam of Kasr el Bint (Maiden's Castle) which, it is believed, was built by the Jews of Khaibar over fifteen hundred years ago. The original structure was about five hundred feet long and is made of basalt blocks. There is no sign of sluice gates and it was no doubt used as a dam and not for irrigation. The remains of many small dams and aqueducts are found in these parts, for the Jewish kings of Khaibar irrigated the whole of the area in this way.

Twenty miles farther on was the town of Khaibar set between two great tongues of lava. Immediately below, a deep wadi, solid with palms, opened to a wide basin in which were more palm groves and the various communities of Khaibar. Beyond the deep cleft of the wadi was the old castle of the Jews, set on a buttress. The wadi is swampy with many springs which breed malarial mosquitoes. Doughty visited the town more than once and had little love for it or its inhabitants. He mentions the inhabitants' dark skin and it is believed that many of them are descended from African slaves. 'Khaibar,' Doughty said, 'is a place renowned in the Moslem chronicles as having been first conquered in the beginning of the religious faction of Mahammad. Khaibar is fabulously imagined to be yet a strong city (which is manifestly never more than a village and her suburbs) on the farther side of the desert; and whose inhabitants are a terrible kindred. Moslems outwardly, but in secret cruel Jews, that will suffer no stranger to enter amongst them. In the midst of the town as they tell, is a wonderful fortress, so high, that even in summer sun cannot caste her beams to the ground. And that cursed people's trade is fabled to be all in land-loping and to be cutters of the Hajj. Also in their running they may pass any horse; so swift they are, because the whirl bone of the knee is excised in their childhood; by nature they have no calf under their shanks . . .'

But that was eighty years ago and we saw no such creatures as we came to a halt near the dingy square of as-Shuraif which lies south of the Citadel. A recent community has grown up along the high ridge above the ancient settlements in the wadi. The men went in search of the Emir and I wandered through the narrow streets wondering just where Doughty had stayed and marvelling at the resilience of such travellers who, despite constant personal danger, continued to keep up their spirits and powers of observation. On the north side of the square was a row of tiny shops and in one of them I bought a white dishdasher for nine riyals (13s. 6d.). Several people gathered to help in the purchase but they faded away when my companions returned. One becomes more isolated when travelling in a group as folk tend to leave one alone.

The Emir was away and we were advised to leave the oasis before nightfall because of the mosquitoes, but first we drove down into the wadi and came to Bab Khaukha, a covered passage which runs beneath a large building near the Marhab cliff. Leaving the vehicles, we climbed the steep sides to a platform in front of the castle. The villages of Khaibar stretched along the wadi and basin, Qariyat al Bishr (where Doughty stayed), Umm Kida, Buwwan, Natah, abu-Washi, al Majda and al Wadi. Along the skyline above the basin are many roofless shelters of rough stone blocks that are used by the bedouin for camping when they visit Khaibar each year. Some come to collect their share of dates, wheat and millet, for they are still part owners with the locals who farm the ground.

The Jewish population was attacked by the Prophet at the village of Umm Kida which we could see two miles to the south-west, and tradition has it that in the cemetery near Qariyat al Bishr are buried the Moslems who fell during the battle. The castle, despite its magnificent position, is un-occupied now and used mainly as a store and for drying hemp. The sun was beginning to sink as we moved off, but there was little beauty in the grey scene.

Riad, who had done the journey before, now became our guide and thirty miles from Khaibar we left the track and turned west again. We stopped almost immediately to camp for it is wise to be settled before dark in areas where there are serpents and scorpions.

Meals were difficult, for the men had no cook and their stove and cooking utensils were inadequate for a party of six. Ali should have been our cook but he was Embassy trained and insisted his job was to drive; also he was sulking for we were travelling too fast, whisking through villages and seldom stopping for tea. Each meal became a scramble as we all tried to cope, for the more people in a party the more difficult it is. The men's elegant stove didn't heat and blew out at the first breeze, so my small Swedish petrol stove and a wood fire were used. His Excellency, whose tummy needed 'watching' drank many glasses of tomato and orange juice from tins and regarded our concoctions with caution and reserve. To be free as I am from the necessity of regular meals and to have a 'cast-iron stomach' are the two greatest assets for any traveller. Finally, with the help of a tin-opener, cheese, tinned fruit and biscuits, we were reasonably replete, and could enjoy the peace of the evening. Later we made up our camp beds beside the vehicles; only Ali felt the cold and slept in the Land-Rover.

Galat Zumurrud

Next morning we searched for some time for Jebel Ghaylan, a small outcrop with a hole through the centre which makes a distinctive landmark in an area where there are no tracks. It was beautiful wild country of red hills, sand and a fair covering of bushes and trees. When we hit the rails we were just south of the station of Galat Zumurrud which is built beside one of the country's oldest wells. The rail tracks run in a straight line across a flat plain which is fed by several wadis from the surrounding hills. The rail embankment is raised several feet above the surface of the plain and any rolling stock must have been an easy target. There were several areas of twisted rails and viaducts which had been completely blown away and the plain was obviously the scene of a big battle. The blockhouse at Sahl el Matar was also badly damaged and near by was a huge pile of bolts and nuts, some of which we took, tourist fashion, as mementoes and set off towards the rising line of hills to the north.

Over this area there is a good supply of sub-surface water which if worked could make the land very fertile as it was in ancient times, so that the project of opening up the railway is not so impractical after all. And despite the difficulties, physical and geographical, the work still goes on; the persistence and continuance of an ideal that will re-open a way that is almost as old as time.

14

Madain Salih – Tombs of the Nabataeans

When the daughters of some lone tents must go herding, as
the Midianite daughters of Jethro, we have seen, they may
drive their flocks into the wilderness and fear no evil;
there is not a young tribesman (vile though many of them
be – but never impious) who will do her oppression

– DOUGHTY

'ULA LIES twelve miles south of Madain Salih and the eastern
cliffs of warm red sandstone protect the oasis which has many
palm groves spreading out into the wadi. Even in ancient times
it was known for the quality of its dates and for the lush growth
of the lemon trees, as it is today. It is a quiet enclosed little
oasis of high mud walls, sandy alleyways and the stillness that
comes from lack of traffic though bicycles are used up and
down the sandy alleys, and there is an electric plant. Some of
the houses have two storeys which are built as a precaution
against flooding and some repairs have been carried out with
the help of iron sleepers from the rail tracks. Incorporated
also in the houses are pieces of stone with fine old carvings
that have been taken from the ruins of the Thamudic town of
el-Khreyby which lies a couple of miles from the oasis near the
east cliff.

Ibn Battuta the Arab traveller visited 'Ula in A.D. 1326 and
he speaks of it as being large and beautiful with palm gardens
and fine well water: 'In the settlement,' he said, 'dwelt
Christian traders from Syria, from whom the pilgrims, who
spend four days here, bought various wares. Nobody did any
harm to these Christians . . .' Today the inhabitants were
friendly but disinterested. We filled all our containers with
water from the spring which now has a good twentieth-
century tap.

The Fabulous Skyline

We crossed the wadi towards the red cliffs which rise sharply and have been eroded into many fantastic shapes. At the intersection of a smaller wadi lie the ruins of el-Khreyby that cover a large area and are now little more than a series of great mounds. Amongst them is the *helwîat en-Néby*, a round cistern cut out of solid rock in the wadi bed which measures twelve feet across and has steps leading to its base, inside. So much of interest to the archaeologist must lie beneath these great mounds, as well as clues and facts which would make it possible to learn more of its early history. Along the face of the cliff and above flood level, are a series of caverns hewn from the rock, and with Himyaritic inscriptions. Many are small, used perhaps for individual tombs and some have been hewn at an angle, to face the setting sun perhaps? On the flattened stone above a smaller ledge, were carved tablets, Egyptian in character, which had a feminine quality that could have been monuments of the harem.

North from here the wadi becomes turbulent for it narrows, and we crossed a jumble of sandhills and rocks into Wadi Hashish. There was a shimmering haze from the slanting sun and as the ground levelled out the wide, shallow valley of Madain Salih lay ahead, golden in the softening light. Far hills form the fabulous skyline of Jebel Ethlib which are rocky spires, pinnacles and crags that pierce the sky like a row of giant penguins, watching our approach. We drove towards them, passing several herds of goats with black figures in attendance. In the open base of the valley were small outcrops of yellow sandstone and on each of them one front had been flattened and carved in ornate design making a façade for the tomb behind. The isolated position gave an affect far more dramatic than the series of carved tombs that ran along the cliff sides. The railway lines ran through the base of the valley to the station beyond where there was a well, the fort, a wagon shed, a few huts and a garden.

Doughty arrived in Madain Salih from Damascus having travelled with a pilgrim caravan. He spent many weeks here whilst they continued to Mecca. What was the quality of this man that he could wander openly in a land where to kill an infidel meant perpetual glory? He was tall with a reddish beard, soft-spoken and with a slight impediment in his speech, good mannered and honest. Above all, he believed in and appreciated each person as a complete individual so that race, colour, position or way of life were merely the trappings. His approach to people whether they lived in his native Suffolk or a rock tomb was the same.

Doughty studied geology at Cambridge, graduating in 1865. He spent ten years in Copenhagen, Louvain and Leyden and during this time he made several trips to Egypt, Palestine, Sinai and Syria. It was during these journeys, having visited Petra, that he heard tales of Madain Salih whose carved monuments and tombs were reputed to rival those of Petra. He set about trying to visit it although the actual position of the city was in doubt and none but the bedouin or those who had made the Hajj could give him any information. He eventually arrived in the Nabataean city in 1876 and stayed in the fort with the Turkish garrison. During the time he made detailed inspections of the tombs and the inscriptions, but his work was done under great difficulty for he was continuously harassed by the bedouin who were far from friendly. Finally he handed over his rubbings and notes to a passing merchant to be delivered in Damascus to the British Consul, and he threw in his lot with the bedu who had befriended him, and made the epic journey to the Najd, Taif and finally to Jeddah. The notes were delivered to Damascus and the book which was to become a classic was eventually written. One needs few other books when wandering through this part of Arabia – small wonder that Lawrence said of it: 'A book not like other books, but something particular, a bible of its kind.'

It is natural to compare Madain Salih with Petra for they were both capitals of the Nabataeans and their cities remain carved out of the rocks. The northern capital of Petra lies in an enclosed wadi and because of the sombre grey-red rock it can look oppressive at times, but Madain Salih spreads over a wide, shallow valley and the yellow sandstone hills, the jaunty outcrops, and series of strange peaks, have a fantasy and gay beauty that surpasses its famous sister city.

Madain Salih came into being, it is believed, when Ad defeated Thamud in Arabia Felix, and he fled north and came finally to the plain of el Hajr (Madain Salih). He stopped near the mountains of Ethlib and built his city. Legend also says that the rock dwellings and tombs were carved by the tooth of their prince and prophet, Salih, and it was the assassination of this prophet that led to the final destruction of the city. That it was a town on the gold and frankincense route from Arabia Felix, and that it grew rich through the passage and transport of the precious merchandise, as the other cities had done, there can be no doubt. Just as its importance declined when trade was diverted to the sea. Little was then heard of the city – as in the case of Petra – and it became no more than a fable. Five hundred years after its decline, Mahammad passed through the valley and he was impressed by the rock dwellings and the fine carvings and by the beauty of the valley, but he used its desolation, its obvious past grandeur, as an example of those who had rejected the apostles of Allah, and it is mentioned in this text many times in the Koran.

There are two prophets called Salih in ancient Arabia which is confusing. The other one is Salih ibn 'Ubaid whose assassination, legend has it, led to the destruction of Shabwa, though it is more likely to have been by earthquake as in the case of the Marib dam. This is the Prophet Salih who is buried in Wadi Sur near Shibam and who was the grandfather of the Prophet Hud whose tomb is a famous place of pilgrimage east of Tarim.

We stopped at the north-west edge of Ethlib near a defile which runs into the massif, it is a narrow cleft one hundred and fifty feet long leading into the many little hillocks and high mounds which make up Ethlib. At the entrance to the defile is an open chamber or hall cut in the rock which is known as the Diwan. Large pillars stand each side but the cornice has fallen and the open space is half filled with sand. It is one of the few monuments which is not a tomb and was used as a *maglis* for it faces north and is extremely cool. Along the sides of the defile is a conduit hewn from the rock which leads to a small chamber above the Diwan, and there are several carved niches and tablets together with many inscriptions that have become badly eroded. There are also some niches with three carved steli and a single column has an inscription above which reads: 'This is the *mesgeda* (kneeling stone) made to

A'ara great God.' There are many inscriptions and carvings over the inner hillocks and mounds of Ethlib, some half hidden by the piled-up sand and others too high to inspect.

We set up camp near the entrance to the defile, protected by an outer buff of rock, but it was a bad choice for the defile formed a wind channel; and during the night hyenas laughed down on the plain.

West of Ethlib is the rocky crag called Kasr el Bint (The Maiden's Castle) which takes its name from a high frontispiece seventy feet wide carved in the rock above a line of tombs set along the base of the crag. The Kasr is difficult to reach and it is beautifully carved, though little has been removed from behind the small door for she must have been a very little 'bint'. Many of the tombs below have Corinthian columns and pillars topped by ornaments of a more Asian origin. In most cases the entrance to the tomb is a gabled door often not larger than three feet by seven and surrounded by carved casings. Sometimes above the pillars each side and at the apex of the gable there is a carved eagle, but most of the heads have been destroyed either by erosion or the fanatical Wahhibis who believe that any mortal who tries to depict a living creature is committing sacrilege, for only Allah can make anything that lives. Most of the chambers behind are plain square cells, some not even tall enough to stand upright, and with niches dug in the sides and on the ground for burying the dead. The tombs continue right round the base of the crag and most of them have names or a history. There is a tomb of the Bint's father and another is the mass grave of the soldiers of the Sheikh.

In the centre of the valley there are many smaller outcrops where the seasonal floods have washed the sand high against the façade. One tomb was less than half finished, the top of the gable and the surrounding stone had been quarried to the same level, whilst below was the natural rock, showing that the Nabataeans worked both niche, bay and monument from the top and at the same time.

Farther to the west is Beyt es-Sany, (The Smith's House). Legend has it that the Smithy seduced the daughter of the Sheikh who sent his soldiers to take vengeance, but the mighty

Smithy met them with his spear and killed them all, and so they are buried in a mass grave.

The most enchanting are the single tombs set on a small outcrop of sandstone with the wide valley setting off their carved precision; and farther to the west are the monuments of the 'City of Salih' where the face of the hills is deeply indented and irregular with many bays in which an entire semi-circle of tombs are set in a pocket of sand. Here we found eagles topping the gables and pillars and some epitaph tablets not yet carved, or so badly eroded they were indistinguishable. On our way back we found pieces of pottery and glass in the centre of the valley.

Perhaps the most beautiful of all the monuments is Beyt Akhreymát, for the base of the side pillars has not been carved entirely away, though the whole form is already there. The pillars merge into the living, natural rock giving a unity and kind of belonging the others lack. It is also the only tomb that has an upper layer of four extra pillars between the mural cornices. There is no bird or ornament on the central pedestal but the remains of badly broken griffins on the side pillars.

The great Mahal el-Maglis stands alone; it is forty feet wide and has a solemn simplicity, with a double pair of pillars not seen on any of the other tombs, a sign of distinction perhaps and fitting for the Senate; and the crude little cell-like interior seems hardly adequate for the grandeur and size of the façade. On the title plate above the gable is a single line that reads 'For Hail son of Douna and his descendants'. The gable and the pillars are unfinished and on the ground near by are the blocks levered from the cliff side and not yet taken away. These signs of unfinished, arrested work which have stayed for centuries are very touching.

There were sockets in some of the surrounds where doors had hung and occasionally a façade had nail holes where wooden cornices had been plugged to cover faulty stone. But now there is no wood, marble or attached decorations of any kind, just the living rock which does, as Doughty says: 'suffice them to "write with an iron pen for ever" upon the soft sand-rock of these Arabian mountains'.

There is a large shed at the Railway Station and inside a

solid, undamaged engine remains as it has for fifty years. The sun pierces the skeleton roof, for every piece of corrugated iron or roofing has been removed and nothing but the giant framework remains. Through an arch the peaks of Ethlib show against the sky enfolding their tombs and carvings as they have done for two thousand years. The blockhouse is large and important and the garden, liberally watered by the good spring, has attracted many bedu who camp near by. We filled our containers with water and wandered through the garden which has vines growing over high trellises making shady places to sit. Palms had also been planted along the rail and one senses that Madain Salih is preparing to be 'discovered'.

As the rail leaves the valley there is the sandy pass of Mabrak an Naqah which lies between two cliffs and here, legend has it, a cow-camel of the Prophet Salih miraculously born of a jebel, was killed by bedouin. From that time pilgrims passing the spot shout and make noises to drown the groans of the dying camel who would otherwise frighten their own beasts. We left the rails turning east to Hadh Hamar to rejoin the Medina-to-Taima road again, and drove for seventy-five miles, a rough but pleasant run for there were no tracks and we found our own way over rocks and through pockets of sand. As we neared the main road, Riad motioned me to stop. Around us stretched a plateau known as the Jaharan Plain.

'You see now,' he said, 'just desert, but after the rains it will come to life; then it will be fine pastureland and you will see thousands of bedu here – thousands. They come from many miles away. It is a fine sight!'

Ten miles from Taima (the Tima of Genesis), is Jebel Ghunaim where there are the earliest written inscriptions, records, to be found in north Arabia. Ahead lay Taima itself behind grey walls where palms showed with a deep persistency. Spreading far out like a great ripple are the fallen ancient walls and to the south are the ruins of the city where King Nabonidus of Babylonia, father of Belshazzar, spent most of his reign, for such was the wealth and grandeur of Taima in those days that he was content to leave the ruling of his own country to his son. Now it is a small oasis in three sections and the landscape surrounding it is dim and grey; but there is an ancient well and the oasis is still famous for the sweet flavour of its dates. A branch of the ancient route goes north-east from here to Syria and Iraq. Taima has always looked towards the east and although she readily submitted to Mahammad when he made his journey north from Medina the town maintained an uneasy independence. Towards the end of the last century the inhabitants owed a loose allegiance to the Rashid Ruler of Hail in Najd who was the last enemy of the Sauds and when the régime fell to the Sauds in 1921, Taima was left in a vacuum until the murder of the Governor in 1950 when Prince Khalid as Sudairi, then Emir of Tabuk, arrived with a force to restore order, and the murdered man's cousin who had taken control surrendered. From then on Taima became part of the Saudi Arabian administration.

The dense clusters of palms rose solidly above the grey walls. The sparsely populated village was withdrawn into itself, its glory tumbled around it like one of the women's dusty black skirts, but in another land thousands of miles away there is something of great beauty which was part of this village, this scene, for in 1882 the Alsatian explorer Charles Huber bought for a few shillings the famous Taima stele, one of the most valuable Semitic monuments ever to be found and which is now in the Louvre.

My companions were behind their tight schedule and we pressed on towards Tabuk. The road crosses the mud flats of al Mahajjab and follows the line of Wadi Qalibah to join the Al Jauf road where it turns due west. Far to our north lay the Sharaura range with the distinctive pinnacle of the Prophet's Pulpit rising above, and ahead of us great bushy eucalyptus trees topped the buildings of Tabuk.

Tabuk is the Thapaua of Ptolemy and her size increased or diminished according to the fortunes of the country's trade, for her one great asset has always been the fine and perpetual springs of water. Locals will tell you her name is derived from the time of the Prophet's visit when on seeing one of his companions digging in the sand to clear a spring, inquired: '*Mâdhâ tabûkûnahu?*' (what are you delving for?). True or not, a peace was arranged with the inhabitants, on condition they pay the *gizja* which was the tax levied on Christians and Jews, so that no doubt it was once a stronghold of Christianity.

We drew up at a police check-post on the outskirts of the town and were directed to the Emir's offices in the Government Administration building. A new square had been laid out, surrounded by new buildings that contrasted with the old Turkish-built suk that continued from the north edge of the square. The Administration building was low and covered a large area, for as well as the civic offices and those of the Emir, there were reception-rooms which in Philby's time had been used as guest rooms for passing travellers. In the Arab way we had stopped, washed and changed into clothes less dusty and crushed before reaching the town and now we sat, a little self-conscious in our unaccustomed tidyness waiting for the Emir. The reception-room was fifty feet long, heavily carpeted and furnished with bulky modern armchairs set around the walls. A large desk stood at one corner. The Emir, dressed in a snow-white dishdasher and kuffiyah came sailing into the room; he was a member of the Sudairi family and greeted us in a friendly manner. Coffee was served and whilst he talked several people came into the room with papers to be signed, or to discuss some urgent matter.

Because of the good water supply and settled conditions, Tabuk is becoming a prosperous farming district. When Doughty visited the area it was a village of forty houses and the inhabitants were permanently harassed by the fierce Atiya tribe who also carried on continuous war with the Turkish officials and soldiers concerned with the pilgrimage. It was not until the country was united within the Saudi régime that the local inhabitants enjoyed any kind of safety. Since that time the Emirs have always been members of the Sudairi family and the previous one was Prince Khalid as Sudairi who spent nine years working to improve conditions, he organized the water supply for irrigation and more and more land was put under cultivation.

The men spoke of their intention of going north-east to Jauf before returning to Jeddah; the Emir regarded me with the look of one in authority prepared for any eventuality. 'And the sitt?' he inquired, 'does she go too?'

The Guest House

Once I was alone it was my intention to go south again, this time following the railway as far as Madain Salih if possible.

'Afterwards,' I said to the Emir, 'I hope to continue north, following the direction of the old route. . . .'

But he knew all about it and called for pencil and paper to draw maps of the two routes which were used. One went north towards Ma'an and the railway follows this route; the other turns north-west and crosses the Midian to the Gulf of Aqaba.

'I shall give you a good guide, he travelled with Philby,' he said at last, 'but now you are all my guests and I shall send you to the Guest House.'

It was a modern bungalow set behind high walls and with an iron gate. There were two reception-rooms and four bed-rooms, each with a number of beds and a bathroom with a shower, though the taps and shower did not work. Maintenance to modern amenities is not yet appreciated; perhaps it is because the older things were made to last and being simpler there was less to go wrong.

The companionship of the earth and nature that had been with us for so long in the solitary places retreated now and the activity of the town took over. We were drawn to the older part where we found the Hajj Qala which had been built to protect the pilgrims and near by was 'Ain as Sudair whose waters still feed the palm groves beyond. A few soldiers remain in the old fort and they took me to the upper gallery where the view was, as they said 'too fine'. The fort is built of large granite blocks and is oppressive and heavy in comparison with Kasr as Sudairi the mud fort whose rounded towers and solid simplicity merge so well with the surrounding sand. A small Turkish mosque has a tidy little minaret and a low stone wall, but it is set apart like an unused showpiece and could have been made from children's blocks. The suk has the usual cheerful gossipy atmosphere and air of intrigue with its beautiful old men sitting in doorways and dozing in the shade. One sees, in such places, the merging of the old and modern. There were brass coffee pots, old silks, flashy nylon and equally flashy jewellery, sandals and slippers both plastic and old leather, tinned goods, great piles of dates, cameras, torches, transistors and a neon lighted café selling ice-cold drinks.

At midday we drove to the Emir's farm on the outskirts of the town, for we had been invited to lunch. The surrounding country was flat and the house, a large square building with an enclosure for the animals adjoining, was set amongst fields, ridged for irrigation, and a small plantation of trees and striplings. We climbed from a bare white hall to the upper floor or roof and a spacious enclosure overlooked a square pool enclosed in extremely high walls. A strong jet of water was filling the pool with water. There is great force in the springs around Tabuk and it would seem that the pressure that caused the ancient volcanoes to erupt still exists.

The Emir sat on a carpet at the end of the enclosure together with his secretary, a member of the Agricultural board and a sheikh of the Atiya tribe. Coffee was brought in by a tall askari in a long beige-coloured thorb which was tightly belted. Agriculture was the main topic and the planting of more palms, fruit trees and grain, was under discussion, as well as the possibility of extra money being given by the Government for irrigation.

Two men entered and placed a large piece of plastic cloth in the centre of the room. They made several trips bringing glasses and table napkins and rounds of flat bread. Also spoons were brought in for the uninitiated. Finally the two men entered carrying a circular enamel dish which was over three feet in diameter, and lowered it carefully on to the cloth. It was piled high with rice and a lamb that had been cut in pieces and placed over the mound. Surrounding it were onions, kidney, peppers and almonds and over the whole was a thin layer of omelette. Several bowls of hot spicy sauces, and others with ladies fingers, egg plant, tomatoes and salad were also brought in.

We washed our hands in the small entrance where a servant held soap and a towel for us, and then we sat on the floor around the cloth. It was some days since we had a good meal and we ate with gusto, all except His Excellency who found the abundance of food and our boisterous appetites disconcerting. Our host sought out tit-bits for us, the lung is good for digestion and, they will tell you, those who eat the tongue will speak wisely. After the main course the men brought in fresh and tinned fruit, custard and small sweet cakes. More coffee was served and, as is customary, we prepared to leave almost immediately.

The Emir followed us out inquiring if we would like to see his animals and we passed into the enclosure where small rooms led on to an open court. In one room were the Emir's falcons and we were instructed to move quietly so as not to frighten them. Previously they had soft and romantic names but now they are called 'Petrol' or 'Jet'. The old sport is dying but the Arab still regards the falcon and the saluki with great respect and gives them an especial place which is different from other birds and animals. We inspected sheep, goats, poultry and ducks imported from England and Africa, for the Emir was looking for new breeds that would thrive in this part of the world. We drank some warm, sweet camel's milk from the cow-camel; and in a separate enclosure was a small gazelle.

'Oh, how beautiful!' I said.

'You like it?' asked the Emir.

'Oh yes!' It stood, frightened in capture, the clean vivid outline standing out against the dim mud enclosure. I thought of the hundreds of creatures I had seen wild and free leaping across so many desert landscapes.

'Well, you take it,' said the Emir, 'take it – to your home.'

'Thank you, but no,' I said, 'it would not be happy in England.' I could have accepted and let it go free later on; but would it be able to fend for itself?

We left the Emir standing tall and handsome in his white robe and debonair kuffiyah, a most romantic gentleman-farmer, and drove back to the suk to replenish our stores.

The party set off very early next morning, for they had a tight schedule and I, the tortoise, went back to bed. Later I found the guide, Mahammad Daheel Awatt, waiting in the lounge for me. He was elderly and pleasant, and after the initial shock of finding I was a lone female was content to sit in the Land-Rover and answer my questions. His most treasured possession was a copy, in Arabic, of the *Land of Midian* which the author Philby had given him. We set off, going south again and following the railway line across the wadi and plain of Ethil. There were eleven stations or halting places between us and Madain Salih. After eighteen miles we passed the station of Ethil and far to our left were signs of cultivation. Cultivation? So different from our own lush ground, but then if camels were allowed such fine pastures their humps would grow so large and fatty, they would be in danger of breaking in the middle with disastrous results.

We crossed the lower reaches of Wadi Ghudayy and after seven miles came to the station of Hsem Birk. These solid, square and unadorned buildings form a familiar line all the way to Medina, a link which in olden times must have given heart to the many pilgrims moving slowly from one to the other. Not far beyond Hsem Birk was a solitary signpost, pointing nowhere, with the number 1209 printed on it.

'One thousand two hundred and nine – what?' I inquired of Mahammad, 'and where to?'

He shrugged. We were roughly six hundred kilometres from Medina and eight hundred from Amman. Did the distance refer to the caravan route north-east to Iraq? The area, which ran towards the base of the hills, was notoriously dangerous, for travellers were easily ambushed and attacked by the bedouin, and there is a blockhouse about every eight miles along the track. Particularly dangerous was the area around Dar el Hadj (Ar Razal) which is set in a rocky basin and surrounded by sharp black rocks. We were running along the northern reaches of Harrat ar Raha and although forced to leave the railway line we were still in a whirlpool of broken ground made by the junction of Wadis Worob, Mustrabra and al Habbini (the latter coming in from the north-east). Here the railway line makes a wide circle to the east and on high ground stands the station of Mustabaha with a large blockhouse and an ancient reservoir below. The rails curve round to the west again, through a narrow defile called en-Nkejb. As far back as the thirteenth century soldiers surrounded the cut in the hills to guard the pilgrims against the bedouin and it is recorded that the leader of the pilgrims sat and watched them pass; counting his flock, as Aytha had done in the south, perhaps. Or was it to gather dues?

Allah Karim!

After some difficulty I drove the Land-Rover on to the line and, bumping over the sleepers, started towards the defile which became deeper and narrower until finally a tunnel confronted us. We drove cautiously into the darkness and I prayed that it had been cleared of dynamite. We moved along and as the tunnel curved to the left a gleam of light showed ahead. When we cleared the tunnel, high salmon-coloured cliffs rose each side, but the ground fell away from the viaduct to the right which hugged the left side. The track ahead was becoming more and more broken and the drop to our right, deeper. It was impossible to turn back. My companion sat mute, protected by Allah. What, I asked myself, am I doing driving to obvious disaster in the heart of Arabia? As though in answer Mahammad murmured '*Allah Karim!*'

The track was tilting, but a few yards ahead I saw a pile of stones to the left so turning the car I drove towards them. We shuddered precariously to one side, and then with a rush, lunged down into the valley below. Now we were in a rocky pocket of sand! I sometimes wonder, at times like this, just what my Arab companions think; their faces will display no emotion whatsoever and there will be no sudden rush to escape. Was Mahammad at this moment blaming the Emir for involving him in such an adventure? Or questioning the wisdom of Allah? Or is he without the imagination to foresee what a spot we were likely to be in? It is more likely that the sublime acceptance of Allah's will saves him the turmoil of such suppositions. The next hour was spent in moving some of the rocks away before it was possible to turn the Land-Rover, and after four attempts, we climbed back on to the track again and headed for the tunnel.

We lost our way making a wide detour around the defile and these barren hills were devoid of any habitation. But we came suddenly upon Qalat el Akhdar whose wells are noted for their sweet water and so the pilgrims filled every available container and carried it for as long as possible. There is a complicated system of reservoirs around the strongly fortified blockhouse and the valley beyond is the beginning of a fertile area that extends almost to Madain Salih. Legend has it that Job washed in these sweet waters and that the worms that fell from his body were turned to stone; if you look hard enough you will find them – little black ones.

Two stations on, at Dissaad we stopped for tea and still we saw no one; was it so deserted or is it the bedouins' natural cunning of keeping out of sight? A habit that is ingrained in the people for everyone outside one's own tribe was an enemy. Not far away is the boulder known as Hagar-al-Bint which is beloved of the virgins of the Swefle tribe. One of the virgins, forced by her father to marry an old man, fled to the rock on her wedding night, declaring that rather than marry the old man she would take the stone as her husband. When her father heard of her escape he came looking and found her lying on the rock. Seeing blood he searched on the sand for footprints of a man, but found none. Awed by the strange happening he allowed her to go free and so marry the boy of her choice. Now the virgins of the tribe need only threaten a visit to the stone, to be allowed to marry whom they will.

Such stories will soon lose their point and even the bedu women will need no rock to fly to; there will be roads and trains and tourists and new ideas. And we few will remember with surprise, the silent deserted lands seen when young; oddities not known to other generations.

15

The Midian

And whosoever shall compel thee to go a mile, go with him
two.   – MATTHEW V, 4

BEFORE CROSSING the Midian Range from Tabuk to the
Gulf of Aqaba we were going north along the railway to
Dat Hajj which is one of the oldest wells in the area and near
the Jordan border. In the vicinity are the ruins of the Nabataean settlement of Quraiya believed to have been an agricultural centre for the area through which the caravans passed.
It's exact position is difficult to locate and Philby is one of
the few Europeans to visit the site. By covering this area to the
north I would now have followed almost the whole of the
route from Medina to the Jordan border.

From Tabuk the railway runs north-north-west through a
wide sandy depression which is bordered on the east by the
hills of Sharaura. The small peaks of al Ajat stand before the
hills and beyond rises the high pinnacle of the Prophet's
Pulpit which can be seen for many miles and is a welcome
landmark when driving across the plain. On the west lies
Hisma, a rocky plateau which extends from below Tabuk, to
Aqaba and al Rumm in the north. Beyond Hisma, flanking it to
the west is the high Midian, a range of granite mountains in
whose beautiful valleys and slopes lie the answers to so much
of our very early history.

There is no made road north from Tabuk; tracks splay out
over the sandy plain for several miles where vehicles have
searched for harder, firmer ground. The basin of al Mahtatab
extends for several miles each side of the railway line and in the
centre is a station of the same name. Farther on the rail runs
over a series of culverts which drain the waters from the Hisma

plateau to the west. Past the culverts is the station of al Hasm with an isolated blockhouse. The stations appeared rapidly for we were able to move fast, and fifteen miles farther on there was the village and station of Bir Hirmas. Two Italian engineers who were working on the railway asked us to have coffee. They hated the arid country, the sparse austerity and missed the ordinary companionship and warmth of their own people. Also it was an uneasy consignment for there had been hold-ups due to lack of funds and difficulties encountered by the surveyors who were perhaps more cautious about laying rails than their counterparts had been fifty years ago.

'Is it possible to reach Dat Hajj and Quraiya from here?' I asked.

'Dat Hajj of course,' said the fair young northern Italian, 'it is the next station. But you must keep to the right for ten miles as the valley has much sand. After that, turn left.'

They knew nothing of Quraiya and Mahammad went in search of information from the local askari. He returned with the second-in-command who had been instructed to come with us as guide. He was a lean young man with a large rifle who looked at me warily.

'We may be away a day or two, doesn't he want any equipment?' I asked.

Mahammad looked uninterested and the askari shrugged; that it appeared, was the least of his worries.

'If you become lost,' said the Italian engineer, 'send an askari and we shall come and fetch you.'

'Thank you,' I said, and drove off trying to work it out.

The askari gazed intently to the west where the ground fell away into the sand which had become so white it made the eyes smart. 'Wilderness' seemed the only description for such a landscape. At last he motioned me to turn left and we plunged immediately into soft sand. I had a strange sense of unease, as though we were leaving the world and its people, driving into the past; and from the moment we turned towards Dat Hajj until we drove away, everything has stayed indelibly in my memory; uneventful as it was.

Date palms, chunky and neglected, showed in the haze and

Dat Hajj

we made a wide circle to the south, skirting deep pockets of sand to run finally on to the rails and towards the now familiar station buildings. Near by was a small row of mud huts and the old fort stood on higher ground with a large open reservoir on the north side. Chunky unattended palms grew around it. The stronghold and reservoir of Dat Hajj was established by Sultan Suleiman because of its fine supply of water which lies just below the surface. The reservoir is no longer filled, for the lorries and pilgrims pass to the east. Until recently this was the border post which has now been moved north to Mudawwarah.

We pushed back the huge iron door of the fort and entered the sunlit open court which was littered with rubbish. One fig tree struggled to live and I had a sudden impulse, a wish, to build a garden here and to tend the old fig tree! The stone stairs leading to the gallery were broken and worn and the high rifle slits showed little of the country beyond.

Mahammad looked round uneasily. 'We go,' he said.

'Why?' I asked, 'there must be soldiers over at the station, take some tea and food and have a meal with them.'

So they went off happily, armed with food from the Land-Rover and leaving me under the palms near the reservoir. It was half filled with sand and at the far corner deeply worn steps led to its base. The grooves in the centre told of the hundreds of pilgrims that came to drink and to wash before prayers, at this spot. To the north the horizon, fused by the heat haze, jumped in an untidy mirage, and it was easy to imagine a pilgrim caravan, with its great army of camels filling the scene. They would come, one hundred abreast, moving forward, slowly, like a great lumbering sea; and bringing the mighty padding sound, the hush, of camels' feet. Such a long time to arrive, but the first distant sound, the great pad, the tinkling of metal, the murmur of voices, the song, the occasional 'whoa!'; and the many faces swathed to the eyes. And above all, the colour. They came, surging forward on their way to Mecca. And to this very spot with one such caravan came Doughty the infidel, brave, for he never tried to hide his identity as a *nasrani*, but to whom many of the Arabs gave help and even affection, as well as the name *Khalil* (friend).

The Midian

It was pleasant to be alone, to dream and – to give thanks. I sipped my coffee, well content. But was I alone? I glanced towards the palms whose unattended base formed a deep thicket and a pair of eyes were observing me intently. The eyes blinked. It was a sandy-coloured dog, wild and uneasy who, realizing I had seen him, was alert and ready to be off. We sat for some time and finally, after the passing of some biscuits, he edged along the ground and stayed, regarding me with wary unbelieving eyes. They are the sad ones in Arabia and although they guard the tents and kill foxes, no Arab will touch nor feed them; therefore they are hopeless thieves. Strays would follow the caravans from Damascus to the outskirts of Mecca where, not being allowed to enter, they waited until the caravan started on its homeward journey again. Only the trained Saluki is taken into the house or tent and only he is important enough to be bought or sold.

The local askari was not happy about us going across country in search of Quraiya for he said there was no track and few people, and if we should break down what would happen? However, though he was worried he took no action for he was, as yet, unused to travellers. We set off to the west and were soon hopelessly lost in a maze of ridges intersected with shallow wadis, peaks and outcrops of sandstone. Several times we stopped and climbed a rock to find our bearings, but even then the corkscrew-like wadis made even a compass useless. There must be only one navigator or guide but, as I watched the bland face of the askari, I mentally reviewed our stock of water, petrol and food supplies. Finally we crossed the Masa'd ridge into the wider stretches of Sha'ib al Ghuwail where, because of the sand, we kept to the rocky sides. Several outcrops of rock stood out in the centre and along the base were signs of an ancient settlement with fallen stones that had been buildings, and lower ones which ringed the fields. We drove round a high rock and saw ahead the ruins of the citadel of Quraiya which stand on a huge outcrop in the centre of the wadi. Some of the thick walls had fallen along the summit and over the cliffs, in a mighty cascade, a petrified waterfall.

To the east the cliff rose sheer for four hundred feet, extending north and south but falling slightly. The ground tapered

Quraiya

off towards the west for about seven hundred yards, sinking in the centre where there was a mass of broken and fallen rock which we scrambled over to reach the solid reinforced walls to the west. At the highest point was a tower twenty-five feet square and from it a solid wall ran north to the cliff side and another to the east. The fortification and protection was evident even in the fallen stone and the only places where walls were not necessary were above the sheer cliffs to the north and south. There are four watch towers joined by inner walls though no sign of any buildings whatsoever cover the whole area of roughly one hundred acres. Despite the lack of buildings there was ample sign of habitation for sherds were scattered all over the surface. Perhaps it was a fortified hill used as a garrison to protect the town below, or a place of pilgrimage, or a prison. A prison? Something of its lay-out and atmosphere, its turrets set at regular intervals along the cliff sides reminded me of Wahni, the Princes' Prison Mountain in Ethiopia. Also a ledge, slightly down the cliff side which formed a large semi-circular platform was similar to those on Wahni. Here, however, it was piled high with broken pottery, as though the vessels had been thrown from the parapet above. Mahammad pointed out inscriptions all badly eroded in the soft stone and we traced the form of the town below as it spread out over the plain. These ruins lie on the eastern side of the citadel and in the centre is a bare depression where a lake or reservoir had been. Beyond were the remains of a dam connecting the hillside and the banks of Wadi Quraiya, and far to the south could be seen an intricate pattern of irrigation, formed to utilize all the waters that reached the wadi. The whole area is fed by the uplands of Hisma and Midian and lends itself to such damming and irrigation. If Quraiya is Ptolemy's Ostama, it would have been the important centre for the whole agricultural tract from Dat Hajj to Tabuk, and here before us lay the ancient 'blue-print' for the rehabilitation of this part of Arabia. The fundamental things for any settlement are still the same, and is not Midian near by, with its history of mines and treasure, another untapped source of wealth?

We camped below the cliffs to the east and the men set about preparing a meal whilst I climbed the rocks looking for inscriptions. High in the cliff side was a natural cave with a walled-up entrance that had been partly pulled away and the cave pilfered. It was nearly forty feet deep and at the far end were two man-made cavities which could have been used either as tombs or for storage. On the floor were several bones of animals, brought here no doubt by hyenas. While I was climbing along the steep cliff Mahammad appeared and announced that dinner was ready. He looked relieved when I returned to level ground again.

After the meal we sat sipping coffee. The askari looked round uneasily.

'Are there any *jinnun* here?' I asked.

'*Impkin*.' He looked at me to judge my reaction.

'Good,' I said, 'I think so too.'

'You have seen?'

'*Impkin*,' I struggled with honesty, 'well, not seen perhaps, but sometimes I know they are around. They help me.'

They are the spirits of the Arab world and there are good and bad ones; beloved of the Heavens they come and go, appearing and disappearing at will. Sometimes they are to be found in the sand devils that spiral across the desert, and sometimes they inhabit solitary ruins. If you travel where they are, you should be prepared to accept their eccentricities good humouredly for you never know when you may need their help. They have great compassion also; I looked up at the high cave with its fallen wall of stones and told my companions of one such *jinn*, and of how a man had been travelling in the desert with his wife who was pregnant, and as they were passing through a rocky defile the woman suddenly gave birth to her child. The husband being alone did what he could but his wife died. Knowing the child would also die in a few days from want of milk, he placed them both in a cave with the baby at its mother's breast and her left arm around him. Then the husband filled the entrance with stones and continued his journey.

'*La ilaha Il-la'l-lahu*,' murmured Mahammad.

Months later bedouin of the same tribe came to the spot where the mother and child had been placed and having heard of the burial they inspected the cave to make sure it had not been disturbed. They found to their dismay that a few stones had been removed and outside the cave were the footprints of a small child. Overcome with fear and superstition they rode off and told the husband of the strange find. He made the journey to the spot and looking inside the cave saw a small child sitting by the body of his wife, which had dried up except for her left eye, the left side of her face, her left breast and her left arm. The husband took the child and, burying his wife in the sand, departed.

'God is great!' murmured my companions, 'it is so?'

I nodded. 'Yes, and when he grew up he became a great warrior and they called him "Khalawi" – born of the desert.'

Mahammad and I were on our own again. We had deposited the gloomy askari back at his post and were now running south looking for a corridor which would take us between the ridges of 'Imarat al 'Ajuz and al Dhiyabiya, through Hisma to the mountain range of Midian. To the right, as far as we could see, ran the high flat plateau of pink and grey stone, remote and formidable, for to miss the one entrance and become involved in the sandy pile-up near the escarpment, would be plain suicide in this deserted place. We made several attempts and each time the sand softened and we were forced to return. We had obviously passed the entrance and it was now late afternoon.

'Shall we stop, Mahammad?' I asked my companion, 'is it all right here?'

'*Tamam*,' he said quietly. He was completely at ease with me now and should I go wandering over the wastes of Arabia for months, I doubt he would raise any objection.

I slipped the Land-Rover out of gear, turned off the engine and let it run to a standstill – one place is as good as another in a plain of sand. The air was still and clear. This is my love! A wide uncluttered land where a person once sighted, could take hours to reach you. Far to the left the Prophet's Pulpit stood up, grey with distance; and to the west the hills darkening against the dying light, were topped with an edge of gold. Tomorrow, *insha'Allah* we would cross them and come to the land of Midian.

We built a fire on the flat sand, collecting dry bushes of

rak that lay about, and Mahammad made strong sweet tea which we sipped whilst the rice, flavoured with onions, peppers, ginger and dried fish was cooking. We talked in snatches, enjoying the silence. Mahammad spoke of Philby in that proprietary manner Arabs affect when they have known and admired a traveller. He produced the book Philby had given him from his small bundle and showed it to me with great pride. It was the Arabic edition of Philby's *The Land of Midian*.

'What a grand present!' I said, fingering the pages; and when I handed it back he smiled.

'*You* have it,' he said, caught by my enthusiasm.

'Oh no, it is precious to you,' I said, taken aback, 'but thank you just the same.'

He wrapped it up in an old kuffiyah and stowed it away. Occasionally as he threw a new bush on the fire to flare, the wide darkening expanse around us disappeared in the sudden near, golden glow. We opened a large tin of pineapple and ate the lot; and drank more tea. Life was very good. When it became cold we wrapped ourselves in our rugs and slept until dawn.

There was nothing for it but to continue south until we came level with Tabuk and so join the southern Midian tracks. We saw the palms and eucalyptus trees and the tower of Qala as Sudairi to the east, and soon found the track running due west towards the uplands. The eastern fringe of Hisma as it falls towards the inland basin is known as Lihh, and it is well watered by the plateau and the mountains beyond. This was the land of the kings of the Minaeans, Nabataeans and the Lihyanites and it is little known to the outside world today. A paradise, one would think, for the present-day archaeologist. Is there, I wondered, any connection with the name 'Lihh' and Lihyanite who were, it is believed, the original Midians?

After twenty-four miles the sandstone plateau ran into the hills and we turned north-west towards the mountains. Far ahead stood the high peak of Jebel Lawz and its red-grey summit gave a foretaste of the beautiful colours that were to come. Soon we ran into a vast sandy corridor where sheer red cliffs rose all around us. On the flat surface of red sand other sharp rocks stood up like sentinels, some of them glistening black in contrast. It is a great natural sanctuary, enclosed and incredibly still and an encampment for many centuries as marks left on the rocks by travellers bear witness. Some of the sandstone was eroded into weird shapes and they made a startling picture as they stood, arrested, in the red sand. We stopped at three peaks, '*Al Thulaitha*' for Mahammad insisted there were many inscriptions though I could find none; but Arabia has a fine filigree of ancient inscriptions right down the spine of her western mountains. The place is known as the Naga Basin and is on the pilgrim route from Egypt, for it continues south through the basin of al Na'mi and into the Khuraita Pass to the coast road.

We made our way through the north end of the corridor and came to a green valley heavily wooded with trees and bushes. As well as numerous birds an eagle followed above us. The tips of the hills which towered around us were bronze and purple. A great high cathedral of violent colour.

'What is the name?' I asked.

'Wadi Husp.'

'Are you sure?' I searched my map but could find nothing resembling the name.

'Wadi Husp,' he repeated.

Jebel Hasab rose to our left and with this I had to be content. Mahammad's habit of speaking with a rush made it difficult at times to understand him. But again, he may merely have been saying, 'Do stop asking questions!'

Thirty-three miles from the Naga Basin we came to the rock of Mafraq which stands at the junction of Wadi Sahab and Wadi al 'Aqla. This is the head or source of Wadi Abyadh which is Midian's largest river; it continues north and skirts the whole of the mountain range and doubles back to the west side where it changes its name to Afal, before continuing south to the Red Sea.

Near by was a signpost pointing along Wadi Dahab and this was the track we had been looking for. Now we were leaving the sandstone of Hisma and entering the granite mountains of Midian proper. To our right was *Hidab al Bir*, which according to its name has a well on its summit. We were circling Lawz which rises seven thousand feet and is seen from so many angles. After ten miles we came to another junction where Wadi Zaytah comes in from the east and converges with Wadi Qahazah from the north. A track runs due north from here along Wadi Qahazah to Alaqen and Hinshan and finally to the Gulf of Aqaba but people on this route are considered *miskine* and so we were turning left along Wadi Abyadh and over the mountains. Soon, leaving the wadi bed we began to climb a high rocky pass where a rough track, which was just wide enough for one vehicle, had been cleared through the stones. Broom grew in large patches and the enclosing hills set off their brightness.

The beni Atiya and the beni Billi use these mountains during the summer months when there is no more grazing on the coastal plain, but now we saw nobody and the clear quiet mountains were doubly aware of our passing. We climbed for four miles through the rocks and broom and at the summit the ground fell away to the left and ahead was a backdrop of purple hills. Coming towards us was a white jeep with a European in a white coat driving and a boy beside him. We pulled off the track on to the stones to allow him to pass but the man stopped the vehicle. He was a French doctor on a medical survey and was returning to Tabuk for some supplies.

'Is it straightforward from here?' I asked.

'Yes, mademoiselle,' he said, 'you can continue to Haql and on to Aqaba' – he paused – 'but you – one vehicle . . .' He looked perplexed.

'You are alone,' I said.

He smiled suddenly, *'C'est vrai!* Bon chance, mademoiselle.' He let in the gear and they shot off across the rocky ground.

We drove towards the great purple backdrop. The ground receded all the time until we came to the base of Wadi Suraym where it joins Wadi Abyadh, now called 'Afal'. It had taken us two hours to cover the last twenty-nine miles from the same wadi on the other side of the range. One track continues south from here along the wadi to the ancient capital of Beda and another goes north-west across the mountains to the Red Sea. A hut stood on the far bank, dwarfed to futility by the towering hills around us. We pulled up as a small man dressed in

The Bedu Grave

European trousers and shirt came out of the hut towards us. He confirmed that our route lay north-west over the mountain and pointed to a rough indentation in the steep hillside. His wife was farther up the wadi with their goats and he invited us to stop and have coffee. But Mahammad had become increasingly uneasy as we penetrated farther into the mountains and he urged me to move on. The man belonged to the Billi tribe. I had expected more panache and colour. The Billi's territory covers an area from the Red Sea coast around Wegh to the railway near Madain Salih, and north to our present latitude. Before the Saudi regime, the Shammar under Ibn Rashid, whose territory backs that of the Billis to the east, were bitter enemies and the two tribes waged continuous war, plundering and stealing each other's camels. Finally when both sides had suffered too many losses for the whole thing to be practical, Ibn Rashid sent the Billi chief, Ibn Refâde a valuable sword and ten camels as a peace offering. Whereupon Ibn Refâde kept the sword but returned the ten camels loaded with twenty bags of the best rice.

We climbed towards the last range of hills leading to the coast, with Jebel Buwarah on our left and another distinctive high-domed jebel on our right.

'What is that mountain's name, Mahammad?' I asked.

'Jebel el Horah,' he said, and indicating the wadi beyond, 'Wadi Horah.' He spoke with the usual rush of breath. There was nothing on the map except Jebel Hawara; and yet, some distant echo, Jebel Horeb – the Horeb of the Exodus? Did Moses – who married a Midian, tend his father-in-law's flocks around these beautiful hills?

We passed a pile of stones with pieces of cloth fluttering from sticks along its top. It should have been a Holy Shrine but Mahammad insisted it was a bedu grave. Now a heady scent of the sea met us as we tipped the last rise and began the descent into Wadi Jurfayn, which is a spectacular and salmon-coloured rift in the mountainside. The surface has huge cavities dug by the torrents and we were forced to hug the south bank. We came to a well called Mijayfil half-way down and then the wadi veered slightly to the south and the Gulf of Aqaba came into view.

The Midian

'Hamaydah,' said Mahammad, pointing to a building on the shore below, '*El hamdu lillah!*'

Below us was a perfect crescent of sand edged with palms which would make a fine camping ground. On the hill is a shrine of the saint Hmûd known as Fakkâk al-Mahâbîs who will free prisoners if prayed to. When the German explorer Musil passed through here in 1910 there was a small community of freed black slaves, descendants of Egyptian soldiers who guarded the halting places on the pilgrim route to Egypt. Now there is only one hut which was occupied by two Saudi soldiers. They put rugs on the sand beside the outer wall and we drank tea overlooking the little cove. It would have been nice to camp here for the night but the askari insisted I must continue to Haql a few miles north along the coast where the Emir lived, for I would be expected to spend the night with him.

When we returned to the Land-Rover a small boy was inspecting it, he pointed to the printed card of the 23rd Psalm which is stuck on the dashboard. '*Aish?*' he asked.

I tried to explain; it was part of the 'Koran', and he indicated that I read it. I floundered badly trying to translate and finally lapsed into English because it is beautiful. He listened intently to the unfamiliar tongue; '. . . my cup runneth over. Surely goodness and mercy shall follow me all the days of my life: and I will dwell in the house of the Lord for ever'.

I looked down at the upturned face, the boy's eyes were searching mine, black, intelligent, with flecks of sand on the lashes. We smiled at each other.

'*Tamam?*' he inquired.

'*Tamam,*' I assented.

Haql which is forty kilometres from the Jordan border was my last stop in Saudi Arabia. It lies at the entrance to Wadi Mabrak and has many wells of brackish water which are reputed to cause malaria and fever, thus the saying: '*Haql salab min al-akl*' (Haql is the ruin of reason). The water doesn't affect the palms for they grow in abundance near the beach and make a good cover for the soldiers camped beneath them. The village stands back and the Emir's house was at the far end. As we drew up the Emir, Ibraham Mazier, came to meet us; he was a tall lean man in the early fifties with a grey skin that spoke of malaria. He was shy but greeted me kindly extending the usual hospitality of the Saudis. We passed through a door in the outer wall and into a small court. He had been notified of my arrival when the itinerary was originally submitted from Aden, and he had been waiting my arrival ever since!

The small guest room was very clean with snow-white linen on the bed, a dressing-table and two pictures of the Emir in gaudy frames. It spoke of the woman's touch. Near by was a bathroom with a shower and wash-basin and a very large mirror which suddenly caught my attention; I had not seen my whole face for a long time; it was brown and freckled and looked incredibly healthy. From the bedroom an inner door led to the harem and the Emir's wife came bustling in. She was about twenty-five, full of fun and very pregnant, a condition which she displayed with triumph. Tabuk? I had been to Tabuk – *wallah!* The Emir had another wife in Tabuk and this was the source of much conjecture with her, which confirmed my belief that these marriages can work better if the wives know each other, for they often become good friends; it is the unknown that worries them; but that does not apply only to women in Arab countries.

Later the Emir came in with a large rifle which he handed to me, 'Keep it beside you,' he said earnestly, 'for protection!'

I moved it gingerly to the back of the bed. If brigands came, this was one victim who would not be hitting back!

The Emir, his secretary and Mahammad drove with me next morning along the track. There had been discussions and disagreements about whether the Land-Rover could climb the steep sandy sides of *Ketib al-Mbassi*. Mahammad had protested. There was nothing, he said, the 'gazelle of the desert' could not do.

The steep side of the wadi leading to *Ketib al-Mbassi* was no obstacle for the Land-Rover and after a few miles we stopped and the others climbed out of their own vehicle to say 'good-bye'. Mahammad stood watching me, was there a flash of regret on those rugged features? One never knows. Like the *siyara* of old he had brought me safely to the end of his people's territory. He had taken my gift of money with the usual acceptance and without thanks, but I knew he was content. I thanked the Emir for his hospitality – for *all* the Saudi hospitality which had been so generously given.

'*Fi aman 'Allah!*' they said, standing in a line on the track, and with regret I turned north towards Jordan.

At the Jordan border I was met by English-speaking soldiers. 'Welcome to Jordan,' said one of them, 'will you have some tea?' and already the wheels of another civilization were turning. I could not find my permit and returned to the Land-Rover. Whilst rummaging amongst the papers and films in my middle seat box, I found tucked away beneath everything, Mahammad's copy of Philby's book. He had left it for me, after all!

16

The King's Highway

There *is* a four-leaved shamrock amongst the herbage if you will only seek for it honestly on your knees; there *is* a straight stick in the wood if you will be satisfied with it when found . . . and better be deceived over and over again than sink into that deepest slough of depravity in which those struggle who, because their own trust has been outraged, declare there is no faith to be kept with others.   — WHYTE MELVILLE

As IT was with the countries to the south, Jordan's importance and growth depended on its transit trade but it had the added hazard of always being a barrier between the desert and the various civilizations of Egypt, Syria and the Mediterranean. The people who made a great mark on the country were the Nabataeans, they reigned for over four centuries and protected their caravan trade not only to the south but north along the King's Highway to Damascus. This northern part of the route was the prized and jealously guarded thoroughfare which the people of Edom forbade the Israelites to use on their flight into the wilderness, and later in the second century A.D. it became Trajan's famous road. Today there is a modern sealed road running from Aqaba, through Kerak, Madeba, Amman and on to Damascus.

Before me lay the final stage of the old route that had begun at Bir Ali and moved in indeterminate fashion north along the peninsula; but from here the track was well defined and there has never been doubt about its direction. What easier route also was there for those three men who brought their offerings to Bethlehem?

The Nabataeans displaced the Edomites in southern Jordan in 600 B.C. and they made Petra their capital. They built a fine city, carving tombs and monuments out of the solid rock and it became an important trading centre for caravans going north along the King's Highway and also west to Gaza. The city was a natural fortress for it was enclosed in a deep valley whose only entrance was through the Sik, a narrow and natural defile cut through the mountains. The Kings of Petra grew rich and powerful by trade and the fees they demanded for safe conduct escorts through their territories, here and in the south. The Ptolemys of Egypt who ruled over the rest of Jordan fought to control the country's remaining trade with their rivals the Seleucids of Syria. The clever Nabataean played the two opponents off against each other, and improved and consolidated their own position through these rival disputes. When in 198 B.C. the Seleucids were victorious in north Jordan and Greek settlements grew up along the route to Damascus, the Nabataeans managed to live amicably with the Greeks just as they stayed neutral during the subsequent fights and rivalries between the Jews and the Greeks. When Rome conquered all the Jewish territory in 64 B.C. the Nabataeans immediately bought their independence and continued to trade until finally defeated by Trajan in 106 A.D.

Some of the blood of these astute and diplomatic people still runs in the veins of the people of Jordan whose country came into being again as a wholly independent nation in 1947, and now as of old it has many borders and uneasy neighbours. Recently Jordan acquired from Saudi Arabia eleven miles of coastline south of Aqaba which gives her more room in which to develop her growing town and port; and she has a good open road from here to the northern border leading to Syria; perhaps given a period of peace, history will repeat itself.

It is easy to be beguiled by the veneer associated with the western world. To sip ice-cold drinks on the hotel beach at Aqaba, watch the water-skiers, and sleep in an air-conditioned suite makes one forget the lack of stability, the poverty and the many displaced persons that bedevil the country. The Aqaba of Auda abu Tayi has disappeared beneath the town-planned civic centre; and Wadi Rhumm, brought from its anonymous grandeur by Lawrence, though still retaining its majesty, now has a road that puts it within the reach of ordinary tourists. So that the magic of the untouched, the colour has gone.

But am I not being contrary? Haven't I advocated just this state of affairs as a means of opening up the rest of Arabia? And aren't such luxuries the first buds of any rehabilitation? This is the continuous mental tug-of-war that travellers like myself experience, for on the one hand we want things to stay as they are and on the other know it is not practical in the world today. But it is painful to watch the corruption of transition; and the resulting period of uncertainty, feeling of inferiority and doubt.

The road runs north from Aqaba towards grey and purple desert mountains and across the plain to the right is Wadi Rhumm, the last of the great solitary wadis. Beyond lay the uplands that were already green. Finally I turned to the west towards Petra.

I had been lured in my affections by the golden Madain Salih, and Petra, for all its beauty was slightly shop worn and 'tourist'. Previously I had slept in a cave and dined in a large and colourful tent, but now there is a hastily erected hotel with a cafe attached, and boys with boxes of cooled orange squash wait at various points for the tourists.

It is still necessary for visitors to leave their vehicles and hire a horse and a guide for the journey into the valley from Wadi Musa, but the Curator of the small museum came with me and so we were able to drive the Land-Rover right through the Sik. This great defile is strange and beautiful as it winds for a mile and a half through the mountain. We moved from deep shade where the cliffs rose as high as two hundred feet into shafts of sunlight, and the passage narrowing again, became just wide enough to allow the vehicle to pass. Finally at the last turn Khasnet Far'on confronted us, for this large edifice in classical Greek style stands dramatically facing the inner entrance to the Sik. The whole side of the cliff is carved in soft pink stone, and it was one of the rare times when the late sun was striking the stone, making it a fiery red. If one moves a few feet away from the Sik's entrance at either end it is impossible to see the cleft. Little wonder that when the city's importance waned and its existence was forgotten, the actual location became unknown for three hundred years.

This was the last and the greatest of the many defiles threaded along the route that had made its devious course through the peninsula.

I was recognized by my former guide and regarded with disapproval by the tourists for my dusty clothes. But rising early before the main body of tourists were about or the boys had taken up their positions the valley was still as magical. I climbed to the High Place on the summit of Zibb 'Atup where the whole mountain-top is carved into an altar of sacrifice, and felt again that strange sense of being at the very top, above all. There is also the Urn Tomb in Greek style whose interior was modified by Jason, Bishop of Petra, in 447 A.D. when it was converted into a church; and the Tomb of Kings, wide and jovial and now an especial site for the orange squash boys. The wide amphitheatre near the Sik with its ripple of eroded seats still looks dim and badly placed. But the pleasant little unremarked tombs, the many clefts and the rock hewn steps leading to higher carvings, became endearing again. Finally I climbed to Wadi ed Deir and to the high clearing where the Temple of ed Deir stands looking out towards the great Wadi Araba. Previously it had been my favourite monument and I returned many times; now the magic came back as I looked at the clean, austere façade and felt its solitary air.

My old guide brought me some Nabataean coins and a small dish, and he would take no reward for them. 'Come again, after a long time,' he said. In the early morning on the day I was leaving the manager of the hotel returned £3 from my bill which I had paid the previous evening.

'We think we charge too much,' he said, 'you have come so far to see our country,' and he pressed the notes back into my hand. How can one help but love such people?

The King's Highway continues through the mountains of Edom and near Shaubak is the thirteenth century crusader castle of Monte Realé which stands astride a solitary hill, a mighty ruin which is built of the grey-white sandstone so that

Kerak

it is hardly discernible from the stony landscape surrounding it. The castle is difficult to approach and therefore deserted. Deep in the earth under the castle is a vast reservoir which can be reached from inside by hundreds of steps, reminiscent of the days of siege. Fifty years ago fine forests covered these barren hills but the Turks felled the trees to have fuel for their railroad. Now the agricultural station near by has plantations of small trees which will one day cover the hills again.

It is spectacular country, penetrating deep into wadis Dana and Hasa with high peaks of red and purple sandstone towering above. These great canyons dig right into the very heart of the earth and are humid and lifeless. Above on the plains it is suddenly green and cultivated, where previously there had been nothing but dry rocky waste.

Few milestones are left on the old highway except the staunch castles of the Crusaders who built on strategic positions used centuries before. Kerak, one of the largest, still towers over the valley on a spot that was a continuous scene of battles and was captured by many people since before the Second Millenium B.C. Mesha, King of the Moabites, was besieged here in 850 B.C. by the Edomites, and the Israelites, and the Moslem Empire captured the site from the Byzantines in the seventh century A.D. When the Crusaders built the present castle in A.D. 1136 its great fortifications and stables were large enough to house an army. But despite its grand fortifications Saladin successfully attacked it and the castle fell in 1188. Later it fell to the Egyptians and at the end of the last century the Turks had a large garrison here. Today it looks quite grand and impregnable. The road climbs the mountain over a vast drawbridge and runs through the modern town to the great walls.

The town, which had been a small village on my last visit, is growing up around it and in the valley below, and repairs are being carried out on the castle and the vaulted stables. Now guides wait at the great gate.

If Doughty's *Arabia Deserta* had been my guide in Saudi Arabia, the Bible was the most important book here. Climbing out of the vast Wadi Mujib I ran towards Dhiban, the Dibon of the Bible where the famous Mesha stele was discovered. Relics that go back to the early Bronze Age have been found during excavations all along the route but here, as at Madeba of the Exodus, all traces are being lost in the growth of new towns.

Amman is spreading over the seven hills that surround the city and it has had as many names as it has hills, for each conqueror gave it a new one. It existed as a settlement in prehistoric times and was the capital of the Ammonites from 1200 B.C. to nearly 600 B.C. In the third century of that era it was known as Rabbath Ammon and when the Egyptians captured the city they called it Philadelphia. The Nabataeans who held it around the first century B.C. gave it the present name. During the Roman conquest they rebuilt most of the city and many of these ruins still stand today. By the eighth century A.D. it was a thriving city under the Arab Umayyads and Abbasids and then came the decline that affected so many cities along the route and by the sixteenth century little remained but a grand and polyglot collection of ruins. It was not until the Hashemite King Abdullah established it as his capital that the city returned to its former importance. Today it has a population of nearly 400,000 and the modern city is grouped pleasantly around the old monuments, giving it another dimension many newer cities lack. The beautiful Roman theatre that holds six thousand people stands near the main road and there is the Temple of Hercules, the Oleam, the Nymphoeum, as well as the colour and intimacy of the suk.

There is a butcher in Amman who is known to have affected many cures by the 'laying on of hands'. His small shop is in the narrow main street of the old quarter and I finally found it the day before I was leaving Amman. I climbed three steps and entered a box-like little shop which was brilliant with neon lighting. The butcher and his two assistants worked behind two counters one each side of the shop. There was an efficient air of bustle and business. The butcher was dark and middle aged with a quiet withdrawn manner and calm eyes. He confirmed he could help my back and his two assistants set up a screen in a far corner of the shop. The butcher ran his hands down my spine, stopping at the place where, for the whole journey, it had been aching. His hands wavered.

'Much pain,' he said and his hands moved convulsively and not of his own motivation.

Except for the light touch I felt nothing and he moved his hands towards my shoulderblades as though he would stretch my spine. He did this several times and then stood back.

'Come tomorrow,' he said, 'it is very bad. It has been a long time. Too long.'

'I must leave tomorrow,' I said. As I stood up my back felt lighter as though a weight had been removed and the ache, though still there was not so bad.

I thanked him. 'What do I owe you?' I asked.

He shook his head. 'It is a gift from Allah, I do not ask money. You should come again,' and before I had left the shop, the assistants had removed the screen and the butcher returned to his work.

Not far off the modern main road to Damascus is Bosra, the provincial capital *Bosra eski Sham* of Roman times. The Romans called the road from Bosra to Aqaba *Via Trajanus*. A straight Roman road with sections of magnificent arches, leads to the present day meagre village which is built entirely of black granite as the old city had been. In the main narrow street one comes suddenly upon a cluster of old columns and towers and the remains of several ruined churches where the workmanship tells of past grandeur that contrasts strongly with the present squalid buildings. Standing apart is the castle dominating and alien to the village for it is expansive and grand. A series of large connected tower fortresses were built by the Saracens around the Roman Theatre which is one of the best preserved in existence, making a whole massive structure. Over a fosse a bridge leads to a vaulted entrance which again leads to the subterranean passages and out finally to the magnificent amphitheatre which is in the process of being restored, for the Turks built ugly barracks over the entire auditorium. Within the castle's precincts is a mosque which had been a church, for in Byzantine times Bosra was an archiepiscopal See.

Battuta, the Arab traveller, speaks of coming here in 1300

on his way to Mecca and of its being the first stopping place from Damascus where the caravans wait four days to enable the late-comers, the stragglers, to catch up with the column. Now in the season, the hikers can stay in the great hall, as their ancestors had done.

The Curator in charge of the excavations and reconstruction lent me his apartment on the roof of one of the fortress towers – a medieval penthouse – and he spent the night in the village.

After a meal I wandered through the courtyards of black granite, and from the ramparts looked over the flat plain at the dwarfed village where broken columns and arches of another finer civilization pierced the undefined mass below.

'Good evening.'

I turned to see a slight young man with the face of a faun standing near the ramparts. 'I am a Christian also,' he said, 'there are many in Syria. You come, I hear,' he continued, 'from the far south.'

I nodded. 'I have come,' I said with a sudden feeling of well-being, 'from where the Three Wise Men came.'

'A pleasant myth,' he said with mock superiority.

'The Story of Life,' I countered, not to be outdone.

We accept the story of the Three Wise Men and the birth of the Christ, told simply to catch the imagination of a child and take it into maturity with us. But surely we have no right to keep our own Christian story to ourselves, for it has larger implications.

'You think the story has significance?' the young man asked.

'The gifts certainly have, and there are other things; at the time of Christ's birth Sirius, the Star of the East was on the meridian line. Orion was close by and in his belt are the stars known as the Three Kings. And so at this time they came with their gifts of gold, frankincense and myrrh.'

'But why gold, frankincense and myrrh?'

'Well they are symbols of the three things that a "whole" person must give – to evolve, to find himself, or the God within him if you like.'

'Isn't that a little blasphemous?'

The Three Gifts

'Not at all. Everyone is a three-fold being, physical, emotional and mental. *Real* living is the recognition and understanding of these, and so having at last the capacity to give.'

'But how can it be that by giving gold, frankincense and myrrh it creates fulfilment?'

I laughed at his troubled face. 'You, an Arab who speak always in allegories, not to know that! Why gold is the symbol of the material world to be used for the good of us all – God as well. Frankincense is the symbol of purification of the emotional, bringing aspirations and longings.'

'But what about myrrh?' he asked, 'myrrh is bitter!'

'Myrrh is related to the mind and is a symbol of purification through suffering.'

'That is for the Christians.'

'Not at all, that is the whole point. It is also for Moslems, Buddhists, animists if you like. The three gifts are universal and the story belongs to all time, our own included. Perhaps it wasn't mere chance that the Three Wise Men followed the way of the incense.'

'I suppose you are going to say that there will be a new Christ, Messiah, or a Mahdi?'

'Why not? There's nothing new in that, though it's not likely to be anything as recognizable as one of those, more likely a mathematician or an economist. Religion isn't being in a church or a mosque, nor is God – you carry them around with you. . . .'

'You talk like a b. . . Moslem,' said my friend looking out on the darkening plain. 'But I am glad that I met you,' he added, for after all he is an Arab and therefore polite.

Damascus, surrounded by its beautiful orchards and gardens, its underlying fanaticism and its new-world bustle, still has a special air. I stayed for old times' sake at the Orient Palace Hotel which now takes block bookings for package tours, so that one moment the hotel is completely empty and the next full to overflowing with tourists.

A gentle old Sheikh in flowing robes escorted by an equally old friend entered the crowded dining-room; he hesitated, thus giving the tourists some heady local colour. I bowed and he acknowledged me kindly and with dignity, before passing to the far side of the room.

'Well!' said an American, sitting near by, 'you know him! Just what *is* he?'

'He's a Sheikh or an Emir, most probably; and I don't know him.' I added, 'But it is the custom.'

'You don't say!' said my American friend.

I was back in the world of cities and loneliness, and later I walked instinctively towards the suk and market area. I might find my goal, the last gate of my journey. Not any more the shaded acacia tree near a well, or a fort; but a caravanserai perhaps?

Not far from the Street Called Straight I found it; here in the oldest inhabited city in the world. The old Khan al Zait. The massive high arch framed a heavy wooden door that towered above me. It led into a round court open to the sky and surrounded by three tiers of rooms for merchants and their stores. In the centre of the court was a large stone pool filled with water – for who can move one step without the precious liquid? And all around and extending far back to the walls was merchandise; rolls of carpet, sacks of grain, large and small wooden boxes and tin boxes. As there has always been. A heady scent of spices pervaded the whole place. Spices – frankincense and myrrh!

'Sitt?'

A small urchin was looking up at me, his high cheekbones chiselled by the harsh shafts of overhead light.

'Soon we close the door, Sitt,' he said, 'you stay?'

I shook my head and moved off. The scent of the spices followed me out; and the great doors clanged shut behind me.

Index

Index

Index

Index

Index

Index